CRÉCY 1346

CRÉCY 1346

WRITTEN BY
DAVID NICOLLE PhD

BATTLESCENE PLATES BY
GRAHAM TURNER

OSPREY
HISTORY

First published in Great Britain in 2000 by Osprey Publishing, Elms Court, Chapel Way, Botley, Oxford OX2 9LP United Kingdom
Email: info@ospreypublishing.com

Also published as Campaign 71: *Crécy 1346*

ISBN 1 84176 259 8

Editor: Marcus Cowper
Design: The Black Spot

Index by Alan Rutter

Back cover map by The Map Studio

Tourist information by Martin Marix Evans

Colour birds-eye view illustrations by the Black Spot
Cartography by the Map Studio
Battlescene artwork by Graham Turner
Originated by Grasmere Digital Imaging, Leeds, UK
Printed in China through World Print Ltd

01 02 03 04 05 10 9 8 7 6 5 4 3 2 1

FOR A CATALOGUE OF ALL BOOKS PUBLISHED BY
OSPREY MILITARY AND AVIATION PLEASE WRITE TO:

The Marketing Manager, Osprey Direct UK,
PO Box 140, Wellingborough, Northants, NN8 4ZA,
United Kingdom.
Email: info@ospreydirect.co.uk

The Marketing Manager, Osprey Direct USA,
c/o Motorbooks International, PO Box 1, Osccola, WI 54020-0001, USA
Email: info@ospreydirectusa.com

Buy online at:
www.ospreypublishing.com

Dedication

For Peter Nicolle and his family,
a long-lost cousin and a new-found fellow interest.

Artist's Note

Readers may care to note that the original paintings from which the colour plates in this book were prepared are available for private sale. All reproduction copyright whatsoever is retained by the Publisher. All enquiries should be addressed to:

Graham Turner, 'Five Acres', Buslins Lane, Chartridge, Chesham, Bucks, HP5 2SN United Kingdom.

The publishers regret that they can enter in to no correspondence on this matter.

KEY TO MILITARY SYMBOLS

FRONT COVER: **Froissart - Battle of Crécy 1346 (courtesy of The Art Archive/Bibliothéque Nationale, Paris)**

CONTENTS

S wenceslaus

ORIGINS OF THE CAMPAIGN

During the early-14th century France and England were more prosperous and powerful than at any time since the height of the Roman Empire, France being the richest country in Christendom. England lagged far behind in terms of population and prestige, although the country was more united. Not only was part of south-western France ruled by the English king, but Flanders and Brittany were virtually auto-nomous. Both these fringe areas also had close commercial links with England.

In 1328 there was a crisis of succession. Philip IV had died 14 years earlier, leaving the Capetian line apparently secure with three sons and a grandson. All of them died in rapid succession, with the last, Charles IV, leaving a pregnant queen. The French nobles elected Philip of Valois (the nephew of Philip IV) as regent and agreed that, if the queen produced a daughter, Philip would become king. A daughter duly appeared and Philip de Valois became King Philip VI. But the only way to legalise this situation was to adopt the new Salic Law, which stated that no woman could rule France, nor could anyone lay claim to the crown through a female relative. This law also excluded several other princes who could have claimed the crown, one of them being King Edward III of England, whose mother was a daughter of Philip IV. For several years things progressed smoothly enough until a new crisis erupted when Philip VI found it politically necessary to support the Count of Flanders against his old friend Robert d'Artois over the succession to the County of Artois. Robert felt betrayed and so transferred his allegiance to Edward III of England. Not long afterwards a similar situation arose in Brittany when Philip VI ruled in favour of his nephew Charles of Blois, and his rival, Jean de Montfort, consequently turned to Edward.

LEFT **The *Mullhouse Altar* was painted in Bohemia around 1385 AD, several decades after the battle of Crécy. Nevertheless its representation of the Saint-King Wenceslas shows the country's patron saint as a warrior-ruler with the typical 14th-century armour used by Bohemia's feudal elite. (State Galleries, no.1038, Stuttgart)**

RIGHT **'A knight rescuing a captive from a giant,' in an early-14th-century English manuscript. The knightly class saw them-selves as fully armoured cavalry maintaining right and crushing wickedness, which was, as in this picture, often represented as a boorish foot soldier. (*Psalter of Richard of Canterbury*, Pierpont Morgan Lib., Ms. Glazier 24, f. 103v, New York)**

Such constitutional problems subsequently provided Edward III with political propaganda when war finally broke out in 1337; he officially proclaimed himself king of France three years later. The anonymous *Invective against France*, written shortly after the battle of Crécy, maintained the justice of Edward's claim by stating somewhat strangely that, 'Christ is the King of the Jews by right of his mother, therefore let the boar [Edward's nickname] be made king over the French by right of his mother.' The trigger to the outbreak of the Hundred Years War in 1337 was, as in so many previous Anglo-French wars, the unclear frontiers of English-ruled Gascony in south-western France. This time, however, Edward III decided to use his claim to the French throne as a political weapon against Philip VI, while the latter used France's old alliance with Scotland as a weapon against Edward. Each ruler also sought allies elsewhere, notably within the fragmented Holy Roman Empire, which included much of what are now Germany, Austria, part of Poland, the Czech Republic, Switzerland, northern Italy, eastern France, Luxembourg, eastern Belgium and Holland.

The first years of the war were very inconclusive. Despite a major English naval success at the battle of Sluys in 1340, many Englishmen doubted the wisdom of Edward III's aggressive policy towards a country as powerful as France and there was widespread fear of enemy coastal raids. Certainly Philip VI had decided to invest more heavily in naval power than France had done before, even hiring fleets of war galleys from Genoese and Spanish ship owners. Philip VI also undermined Edward's alliances in Flanders, though Edward opened up a new front in Brittany.

By 1345 the war was becoming dangerously expensive for both rulers. Edward III's allies held most of Brittany on behalf of Jean de Montfort. French attacks on Gascony in the south-west had been checked and Edward III had rebuilt his Flemish alliances. Finance was a problem for Philip VI, whose subjects objected to paying taxes unless France was actually being invaded. Edward III also borrowed heavily and widely, so much so that the famous Bardi bank of Florence, lenders to crowned heads across Europe, collapsed when Edward failed to repay his debts in 1346.

Philip VI sent senior officials to recruit a war fleet in Nice, Monaco and Genoa consisting of 30 large and two smaller galleys whose crews could also serve as infantry. Crossbow-armed marines were recruited separately, and in March 1346 a large number were reviewed in the grounds of the Carmelite Convent in Nice. Edward III's preparations were similarly careful, and focused on English troops rather than uncertain Flemish or Breton allies. His officers recruited men, purchased supplies and arms, and requisitioned large numbers of ships. One such order to the sheriffs of Oxfordshire, Berkshire and elsewhere to purchase bows, strings and arrows demanded, 'Since, for the sake of our expedition of war to France, we have immediate need of a great quantity of bows and arrows, we now firmly order and command you ... [that] you shall immediately cause to be brought and provided for us, out of the issues of your jurisdiction, 200 bows and 400 sheaves of arrows, from whatever places may seem best to you ....' They were taken to the Tower of London, where Edward's clerk, Robert de Mildenhale, promised to repay the sheriffs' expenses at a later date.

Secret diplomatic or spying missions were sent to different parts of Europe before and during the Crécy campaign. Philippe de Burton, for example, was sent secretly to Spain and Portugal, along with André de Offord and Richard de Saham. Richard de Saham was subsequently sent to the Islamic Amirate of Granada in 1346-47, so perhaps he was regarded as an Iberian specialist. Other embassies were sent to Germany, Italy, Bohemia and Hungary.

THE OPPOSING COMMANDERS

ENGLISH LEADERS

Edward III was born in 1312 and became king when his father Edward II was deposed in 1327. His long reign seemed filled with foreign wars while the Black Death, the plague of 1348, cast its ghastly shadow over the middle of the century. More positively Parliament also became a major force in English politics. Edward III's early years as king were overshadowed by his domineering mother Isabella of France, and her lover, Roger Mortimer, until in 1330 Edward had Mortimer executed and exiled his mother to a convent. Edward III is said to have been devoted to the ideals of chivalry, founding the Order of the Garter in 1348, but, despite an apprenticeship fighting the Scots, he had personal experience of only two major battle, Halidon Hill in 1333 and Crécy in 1346. His wars saw early successes and ended in long-term failure, while he himself died alone in 1377, his infamous mistress, Alice Perrers, having taken the rings from his fingers while only a priest remained to give the king the last rites.

His son, Edward, Prince of Wales, known as the 'Black Prince', is regarded as one of the most romantic figures in English history. The eldest son of Edward III and Philippa of Hainault, he was born in 1330, and was tall, muscular and a fearsome warrior. Even as a child Edward was given symbolic duties, becoming Earl of Chester at three, Duke of Cornwall at six and Prince of Wales in 1343. His participation in the Hundred Years War began two years later and he was only 16 when he

A scene of knightly combat between Tristan and his foes in the Arthurian cycle wall-painting in a small castle in central France. Its dating is unclear, but most of the arms, armour and costume are remarkably old-fashioned. (St Floret Castle; author's photograph)

The so-called effigy of Bertold V, last Duke of Zahringen, dating from the early-14th century, is well over life-size. The knight's costume and armour are typically German. (Freiburg-in-Breisgau Cathedral; author's photograph)

French eating knife with a carved bone handle, 14th century. (Hermitage Museum, St Petersburg)

earned a reputation as a great warrior at the battle of Crécy. On that occasion his authority was largely nominal, but at the battle of Poitiers in 1356 Prince Edward proved himself one of the finest commanders of his generation. In reality, however, his reputation for chivalry was earned in tournaments rather than on the battlefield, and his nickname of the Black Prince is likely to reflect his ruthlessness rather than the supposed colour of his armour. He fought his last campaign carried in a litter and his illness may have contributed to his savage treatment of the French city of Limoges. He died in 1376, a year before his father; his cultured son Richard II became king on Edward III's death.

English noblemen commanded various parts of the army during the Crécy campaign, William Bohun, Earl of Northampton, probably being the most important. He supported Edward III during the political coup against his mother in 1330, then fought alongside the king in Scotland and Flanders where he earned a reputation for boldness. But William Bohun was more than merely a soldier; he was a member of an important embassy to the Pope, was granted the title of Earl of Northampton in 1337 and became Constable of England the following year. He was one of the commanders of an Anglo-German force that campaigned in north-western France in 1339 and in the early 1340s he served as the king's lieutenant in Brittany, where he won several notable victories before being recalled to help with the Crécy campaign. William Bohun remained a loyal supporter of Edward III, taking part in most major campaigns before his death in 1360.

Thomas Beauchamp, Earl of Warwick, was another leading English commander during the Crécy campaign. In 1339 he had been one of the more successful leaders of a somewhat lacklustre Anglo-German campaign near Cambrai. In 1340 he was sent back to Flanders but with too few men to make much difference. With Northampton he was briefly imprisoned in Brussels as surety for Edward III's debts and in 1342 he too was sent to Brittany. Thomas Beauchamp was a founder knight of the Order of the Garter and, like Northampton, took part in most major campaigns of the Hundred Years War before his death in 1369.

Godfrey de Harcourt was a minor baron from Normandy and is regarded as a traitor in French accounts of Crécy. The Harcourts claimed descent from a 10th-century Viking chieftain and Jean II de Harcourt had been Admiral of France. His eldest grandson, Jean IV, received the title of count in 1338, but Jean IV's brother Godfrey, the lord of Saint-Saveur in the Cotentin peninsula, became a chronic rebel against the French Crown. The immediate reason for Godfrey de Harcourt's rebellion was a dispute with Robert Bertrand, lord of neighbouring Bricquebec, about the marriage of a local heiress. Both were summoned to Paris and during the course of a heated argument swords were drawn in the presence of the

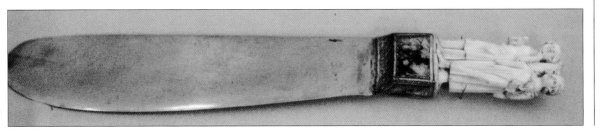

king. Godfrey refused to return to Paris for judgement and gathered support among other disgruntled members of the Norman nobility. When their rebellion failed, Godfrey de Harcourt fled to Brabant and then to England in May 1345. Godfrey is sometimes credited with the idea of invading Normandy. According to the chronicler Froissart, he told Edward III, 'Sire, in jeopardy of my head, if you will land there, there is none that shall resist you. The people of Normandy have so far had no experience of war, and all the chivalry of France is gathered outside Aiguillon [in Gascony] with the Duke [of Normandy, King Philip's son]. And Sire, there you shall find great towns without walls where your men shall have riches to last them twenty years.' After Crécy, Edward's decision to abandon Normandy undermined Godfrey de Harcourt's hopes of returning to his ancestral estates and, after again fleeing to Brabant, he returned to King Philip's court with a rope around his neck, begging forgiveness. Any reconciliation was, however, temporary and in 1356 Godfrey de Harcourt again appealed to Edward III for help, this time against Philip VI's son, King John II.

FRENCH LEADERS

Philip VI was the first French ruler in many generations to suffer defeat at the hands of the English. He was born in 1293 and his father, Charles, Count of Valois, Anjou and Maine, was the younger brother of King Philip IV and a grandson of Louis IX. His mother was Marguerite, daughter of King Charles II of Naples in southern Italy. When Philip himself inherited Valois, Anjou and Maine, his first cousin, Charles IV, was king of France.

Crowned in 1328, Philip VI died in 1350 and was the first of the Valois dynasty, which ruled France until 1589. Philip is remembered as an astute politician rather than as a warrior, and was extremely cautious in military matters. In this he followed the advice given in an anonymous motet, or song, addressed to himself and his son.

> *'Philip, more valuable than iron,*
> *better than force used artfully;*
> *is prudence, superior to large armies, enabling you*
> *to bring back spoils from the enemy.'*

Charles II, Count of Alençon, was the younger brother of King Philip VI. He was more of a warrior than the king and before the catastrophe of Crécy was quite successful. In 1330, for example, he captured the English-held city of Saintes in western France despite its large garrison. Whether his subsequent sacking of Saintes was approved by Philip VI is unclear but it forced Edward III to surrender his previous position. Unfortunately his success at Saintes may have given the Count of Alençon a false impression of both his own abilities and those of the English. Nevertheless, he remained one of the most experienced advisers to King Philip and his sickly son Duke John of Normandy, the future King John II, and supported Charles of Blois in his attempt to regain Nantes, the historic capital of Brittany. Alençon's participation in the negotiations that broke an Anglo-Flemish alliance near Bouvines without recourse to a battle also suggests that he had diplomatic talents.

This picture of a warship carrying mailed troops and defended by an archer and a crossbowman is in an English manuscript made around 1340. (*Luttrell Psalter,* British Library, Ms. Add. 42130, f. 161v, London)

John of Luxembourg was the son of one German emperor and the father of another. He himself was something of a knight errant, a chivalrous figure with skills of leadership and diplomacy, as well as absolute loyalty to France. Bohemia, which now forms part of the Czech Republic, lost its native ruling dynasty with the assassination of Wenceslas III in 1306. The Bohemian nobility then turned to the Luxembourg dynasty, a German family under strong French influence. As a result, the 14-year-old John of Luxembourg became king of Bohemia in 1310. His chivalric enthusiasm prompted his participation in Crusading campaigns in Lithuania (1328-29, 1337 and 1345), campaigns in Italy (1330-31) and in Bohemia itself. John of Luxembourg's own interests were focused firmly westward. His ancestral estates lay in the fragmented western regions of the Empire, bordering France. Here the aristocracy spoke French while the common people spoke a variety of Low German dialects which the French lumped together as Thiois. Throughout his adult life, John of Luxembourg remained a faithful courtier, soldier and diplomat in the service of the French Crown. As one of Philip VI's most trusted confidants, he was given authority in south-western France in 1338-39, fought alongside the king in Cambrai, and formed part of the negotiating team that broke the Anglo-Flemish alliance at Bouvines. John of Luxembourg was also one of Philip VI's main financial backers for the Crécy campaign in 1346, by which time he was not only old, but almost blind.

Count Louis of Flanders was also known as Count Louis II of Nevers 'de Creci' to differentiate him from his father, Count Louis I 'de Flandre', whom he succeeded in 1322 at the age of 18. Separated from his family at an early age Louis was brought up in the French court and had little understanding of his Flemish subjects, whose interests often clashed with those of the French Crown. Louis, however, remained totally loyal to King Philip VI even though this damaged his position in Flanders, and, perhaps as a result, was sometimes described as unimpressive and lacking judgement. Other evidence suggests that Louis of Flanders was not the buffoon history has painted, and he

Squires arming knights who then joust with one another, as shown on a French or Italian carved ivory mirror holder, mid-to late-14th century. (Bargello Museum, Florence)

showed considerable guile in escaping from Ghent when he might otherwise have become a prisoner within his own lands. Thereafter he remained in exile at the French court until his death at the battle of Crécy. He took part in the Cambrai campaign of 1338, strongly opposed a French invasion of Flanders in 1340 because the resulting devastation would ruin his chances of ever being accepted back, and played a part in the highly successful negotiations at Bouvines.

Carlo Grimaldi, Il Grande, was from one of the four leading families in medieval Genoa. The Grimaldis were Guelphs, traditional supporters of the Papacy in its ancient rivalry with the Holy Roman Empire. Thus, by extension, they were friends of France, which had long been the Popes' most powerful supporter. Consequently Grimaldis were often found in French service as mercenaries, naval commanders or allies. Carlo's father, Ranieri, had been lord of the Mediterranean enclave of Ventimiglia from 1329 to 1335 until ousted by a Ghibbeline (pro-Imperial) coup. Four years later the Genoese, tired of the squabbling between their Guelphs and Ghibbeline aristocracy, proclaimed Simon Boccanegra as their new doge, or ruler but, Ventimiglia, where Carlo Grimaldi had regained control, denied the new doge's authority. In 1341 Carlo purchased Monaco from the Spinola family and this, with Ventimiglia and Roquebrune, became a refuge for Genoese Guelph families. Carlo Grimaldi and various members of his family, friends and dependants offered support to Philip of France in his struggle with Edward III of England. The Grimaldis' territory may have been tiny, but their naval potential was significant. They were also prepared to fight alongside fleets supplied by their Ghibbeline rivals, the Doria family. For the first time in its history, the autonomy of Monaco was recognised while Carlo and his brother Antoine were made vicars, or governors, of Provence. In 1346 Carlo Grimaldi was temporarily ousted from Monaco by a local coup, but by then he was fully engaged in providing support to Philip VI, resulting in his own serious injury at the débâcle of Crécy.

OPPOSING FORCES

THE ENGLISH

When the Hundred Years War began, the English Crown could draw upon plenty of professional soldiers in England and Gascony, and many commanders were experienced in combining different kinds of infantry and cavalry. Such capabilities resulted from a virtual military revolution that had taken place during the first half of the 14th century. An important part of this was the indenture system, which, although it had been used earlier, meant that England could field entirely indentured or paid professional or semi-professional armies. At the start of the 14th century the higher aristocracy of England would not serve for money for fear of losing status but by the 1330s all accepted pay. Many of them also became military sub-contractors, raising troops by enlisting or indenturing their feudal tenants and members of their own households.

This did not, however, mean that the men who fought at Crécy were different from those who fought in earlier wars. They merely served under different conditions; they were volunteers who were properly paid for their participation. No indenture documents survive from the Crécy campaign, but in 1341 the Earl of Northampton was contracted to supply seven knights banneret, 84 ordinary knights, 199 other men-at-arms, 250 archers and 200 other infantry soldiers. This indenture system may also have reflected the older Commissions of Array, which listed available fighting men and their equipment based upon the value of

English effigy of an unnamed knight, 1340-50. This effigy is unusual because the figure has a raised, though now very damaged, visor. (Alvechurch Church; author's photograph)

their property. Only a quarter to a third of these levies were listed as archers and most of these were minor yeomen rather than the poorest peasants. Urban levies were similarly much better equipped than those from country areas.

Nevertheless, it seems that there were still not enough voluntary recruits and in 1345-46 unpopular orders went out to enlist men through the old Commissions of Array. Another source of military manpower was men convicted of crimes, and several thousand war-service pardons were issued during 1346-47. The poor and backward Celtic fringes of the realm were a further useful source, Wales providing archers and spearmen, Cornwall spearmen, while assorted troops came from Ireland. All were, however, regarded by both English colleagues and French foes as singularly brutal in battle. Then there were local troops in English-ruled Gascony, as well as Edward III's Breton and Flemish allies, where the wealthy city of Bruges alone could mobilise 7,000 militiamen. Edward III had hoped to raise an army four or five times larger than those previously used in Flanders and Scotland. Although this was not achieved, the army which eventually sailed to Normandy was very large by the standards of the day.

A young King Edward III of England does homage to King Philip VI of France for his possessions in Gascony in 1329, as illustrated in a mid-14th-century French manuscript. Such friendship would not, however, characterise their relationship for long. (*Grandes Chroniques de France*, Bibliothèque Nationale, Ms. Fr. 2090-2, Paris)

English armies were still bound together by a loose sense of feudal obligation despite the importance of the indenture system, and English military organisation lagged behind the systems of France, Burgundy or Italy. Leadership remained a noble prerogative, as did the command structure, which was reflected in the creation of the Order of the Garter, one of the earliest secular orders of knighthood. Like the slightly older French Order of the Star, but unlike the old religious Military Orders, it was intended to focus loyalty upon the monarch rather than the Church.

Military retinues were not of standard sizes, nor were the proportions of infantry and cavalry, archers and spearmen. Leaders led the troops they had, whatever their skills, and the optimum size and composition, though recognised in theory, was rarely achieved. The existence of terms such as *vintenar* (an officer leading 20 men) and *centenar* (a man leading 100 men) suggests that such troops, particularly infantry, were divided into roughly regular units where possible. There is also evidence that at Crécy and elsewhere English-speaking *vintenars* and *centenars* were put in command of Welsh foot soldiers to improve communication and perhaps control their wild behaviour.

The provisioning of English armies was sophisticated. The Royal Wardrobe was closely involved in military matters, while its sub-department, the Privy Wardrobe, supervised the storage of important military equipment including the new-fangled guns. This Privy Wardrobe consequently became a reserve of stores to be used in expeditions such as that of 1346. The main source of food, clothing and military equipment was managed by a system of purveyance, allowing local officials to purchase whatever was needed at what they regarded as a fair price. Not surprisingly, there was widespread corruption and in the year of Crécy Edward III, 'on hearing the great outcry and the complaints common amongst his subjects', punished purveyors who abused their position. During the winter of 1345-46 the Tower of London, Greenwich and several other places served as depots for huge numbers of bows, while food was brought to numerous collection points – there were seven in Yorkshire alone.

The Keeper of the King's Wardrobe Accounts was primarily responsible for army wages during the Crécy campaign, its clerks sometimes accompanying military commanders to supervise payment. At this time a fully armoured cavalryman or man-at-arms was regarded as worth ten infantry. Payment among the cavalry also varied, but the following daily rates seems to be typical of Edward III's time: a duke 13s. 4d; an earl 6s. 8d; a knight banneret 4s; a knight bachelor 2s; an esquire 1s. It is worth noting that the basic armour expected of a man-at-arms at the start of the 14th century cost about six days' active service pay, and armour had become more expensive since then. Additional payment was introduced for overseas expeditions, averaging around 6d per day. Payment for non-noble troops was much less, though military engineers could expect high status and high pay. Even so the pay of a common soldier serving within England might be twice or three times that of a peasant, with additional pay for service overseas. Otherwise, the pay of an archer was more than an ordinary foot soldier, an English archer more than a Welsh archer, a crossbowman more than a longbowman, and a mounted archer similar to that of a non-noble cavalryman.

These paid indentured armies enabled longer-term planning and as a result the first decades of the Hundred Years War saw more co-ordinated movement and multi-pronged attacks than previous conflicts. The availability of experienced military leaders from the upper and lower aristocracy also relieved the king of mundane military concerns. On the ground, however, tactics remained remarkably traditional. On the march English armies were usually divided into three battles or divisions: vanguard, mainward and rearguard, each with their own men-at-arms and archers, their flanks being protected by mounted archers and men-at-arms. Similar attention was paid to transport systems. In 1359, and almost certainly during the Crécy campaign, the main units were preceded by a sort of pioneer corps of varlets who, according to Froissart, 'went before the carts and cleared the paths and ways, and cut down the thorn bushes and the thickets, so that the carts might pass more easily'.

The importance of battlefield tactics has consistently been exaggerated by military historians, as has the supposedly superior English firepower achieved by massed use of longbows during the Hundred Years War. What did change was the number of archers in English armies and a more effective co-ordination between archers in defensive array and men-at-arms, either on foot or on horseback. Such tactics would remain largely unchanged throughout the Hundred Years War and a lack of further development would contribute to England's ultimate defeat. The fully armoured English men-at-arms were now not only prepared to fight on foot, but also co-ordinated their actions with those of the previously despised infantry. By learning to work together, and with their leaders beginning to employ archers and dismounted men-at-arms in concert,

a

b

English armies consistently defeated their French opponents for decades to come.

Despite the dwindling number of militarily active knights in England, Edward III was never short of men-at-arms. There were probably four non-noble men-at-arms for every person of knightly rank or above, while there were still enough men of aristocratic rank to fill command and leadership ranks. In fact many from knightly families remained as squires because of the huge expense involved in full knightly status. William de Thweyt, for example, the younger son of a Norfolk gentry family, took up a military career, fought at Sluys and Crécy, and commanded garrisons in England and Ireland. Such men formed the seasoned backbone of King Edward's army. But the English population no longer seems to have held the knightly élite in particularly high esteem. *The Romance of Sir Percyvelle de Galles* was probably written in the north Midlands for a non-noble audience during the mid-14th century. It gently mocks the knightly way of life, its self-importance and its limited usefulness in battle, as in one part of the poem where a heroic knight has to raise his visor to see what is going on:

> *'And fast going they flee; for he was so mightily clothed [armoured]; all fearful from him they fled, and ever the faster that they sped, the swiftlier he came, until he was aware of a knight. And when of this manoeuvre the knight had sight, he put up his visor on height, and said, Sir, by God watch out.'*

For its part, the English knightly élite regarded the master at arms or professional military teacher as suspect, while fencing was seen a 'trade of subtlety undermining true and natural valour'. Mercenary cavalry played a prominent role in Edward III's armies: German men-at-arms were recruited by the English more than by the French, while men from Savoy served on both sides. Another unusual form of cavalry was the hobelar, a light or almost unarmoured cavalryman riding a small fast horse or pony. They served Edward I in Ireland in 1296 and English hobelars were mentioned four years later. From the 1330s they served alongside mounted archers, who were themselves first recorded in 1333.

English historians have largely focused on English infantry during the Crécy campaign. The most effective element was, of course, the long-bowmen. Modern archers have shown that a longbow could be shot 15 times a minute, and although this was far slower than the rate of oriental archers, who used composite bows, it was much faster than the best cross-bowman's rate of shooting. A fully trained 14th-century longbowman would also have done better. At home archers practised against targets at a range of around 225 metres. In battle they could shoot with an almost flat trajectory at a close-range target to achieve maximum penetration, though their greatest success at Crécy seems to have been by shooting indirect with a high trajectory to drop arrows within a designated killing zone. Such indirect archery did relatively little harm to fully armoured men, except to their less protected limbs, but the arrows caused havoc to horses as even the best horse-armour was still largely made of mail, felt or padded material. The function of an English longbowman when using zone shooting was, of course, the same as that of Byzantine or Persian horse-archers while shooting at rest – namely to dissipate the striking power of an enemy cavalry charge.

The English mounted archers, of whom 1,700 served in Brittany in 1342, were not horse-archers but were capable of keeping up with the cavalry men-at-arms with whom they formed a mobile striking force. In the early part of the Hundred Years War most mounted archers came from towns rather than rural areas, more from southern England than from the north or the Celtic regions. It is also clear that prosperous yeomen families could supply both mounted archers and non-noble men-at-arms. Much less is known about the so-called spearmen who fought throughout the Crécy campaign, except that their status and their pay was low. Many came from Cornwall or Wales, and those from north Wales in the service of the Prince of Wales or the Earl of Arundel were the first units in Edward III's army to wear proper uniforms. Arundel's men wore red and white, the Prince of Wales' green and white.

The English fleet was not a navy in the modern sense and was far less disciplined than the army. But by the mid-14th century its technology was more sophisticated than is generally realised. Fishermen from the British Isles sailed far afield, perhaps almost as far as those Scandinavian mariners who took identical ships to Iceland and Greenland. On the other hand the psychological horizons of English sailors were much more limited than those of the Genoese, Spaniards or even the French. It was almost impossible for their commanders to keep a fleet together for any length of time, or for individual vessels to maintain station in

ABOVE **Part of an early-14th-century stained glass window of the Tree of Jesse, plus a series of donor figures. The armour is very old fashioned and could even date from the late-13th century. (Church of St Mary, Shrewsbury; author's photograph)**

BELOW **Part of a large, richly embroidered textile showing the golden leopards of the ruling Plantagenet family of England, on an essentially red ground. It was made between 1325 and 1350 and may have been part of a horse's caparison or covering. (Musée de Cluny, inv. Cl. 20367, Paris)**

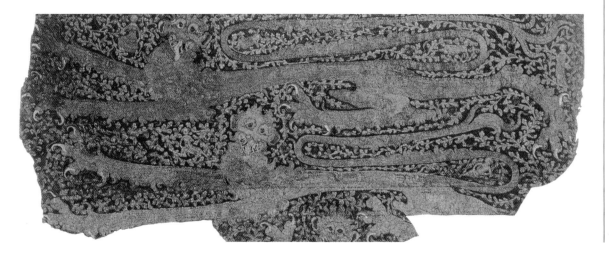

relation to one another. In fact the men who actually fought at sea for Edward III, rather than merely controlling the ships, were soldiers rather than sailors and this was particularly true of their commanders.

Most ships were commandeered or 'arrested' when needed for royal service. They came from all around England, principally from the southern and East Anglian coasts, their crews and ship-masters being paid from the Royal Exchequer via the masters of their home ports. The only permanent naval arsenal was at the Tower of London, where the Clerk of the Royal Ships had his office. The king also had a few royal ships, either purchased or captured from the enemy, although most seem to have been specially built. Nor did these vessels have permanent crews, which were hired, press-ganged or selected from jail when needed.

The 14th century was a time of great change in armour, though less so in weaponry, with an increasing use of French terminology, reflecting new pieces of equipment. In *The Lay of Havelock the Dane*, probably written in Lincolnshire early in the 14th century, most items of armour had names

derived from French with only the simplest or most basic having Norse or Anglo-Saxon names. More French terminology is seen in a version of *Sir Gawain and the Green Knight*, written in Cheshire around the mid-or later 14th century. Archery mostly used English terms except, interestingly enough, for the barbe or barb of a war-arrow. Other infantry weapons are mostly English or Norse but, as in *The Lay of Havelock the*

One side of the wooden Levitic Pew end, mid-14th-century German. This carving is particularly important because it illustrates the rear as well as the front of a coat-of-plates, here with two shoulder buckles and two buckles on the back. (Verden Cathedral)

St George and the Dragon, a Bohemian wall-painting made before 1350. Though old fashioned, this picture shows the basically German-style military equipment used by the knightly élite of Bohemia around the time of the battle of Crécy. (The Melantrich House, Prague)

Dane, the French giserne or gisarme is mentioned. *Sir Gawain and the Green Knight* also included a detailed description of a knight putting on his helmet:

Then lifts he the helm and hastily it kisses; that was stapled stiffly [referring to the vervelles, which secured the mail aventail] and padded within. It was tall on his head, buckled behind [to his coat-of-plates]; with a fluttering vrysoun [cloth covering] hanging over the aventail; embroidered and bounded with the best gems; with broad silken borders and birds on the seams.

Longbows were not, of course, new but had largely fallen out of favour as a military weapon during the 13th century. In fact the longbow was simply called a bowe until the 16th century and was widely used in the Low Countries, France, Scandinavia, Italy and elsewhere. Its draw-weight was usually between 30 and 46 kilograms and, though it could rarely penetrate the armour worn by the 14th century to protect the vital organs, it could inflict disabling wounds to limbs and to horses. The best arrows were of ash, though many were of aspen, and they included different weights for long-range flight shooting, ordinary archery, and arrows with heavy broad heads for use at short range. In 1347 such bows were 1s 3d each, with a sheaf of arrows costing 1s 4d, a high price compared with the wages of an ordinary working man or peasant. The numbers of bows and arrows needed for campaigns like Crécy was enormous, requiring the importation of raw materials from much of the known world. In 1341, 35 counties supplied 7,700 bows and 13,000 sheaves of arrows. In 1359 the same areas sent 20,000 bows, 850,000 sheaves of arrows and 50,000 bowstrings to the Tower of London.

Other weapons ranged from the simple cultellus, or knife, worn by men of all classes, and the broader-bladed basilard dagger, which reached England in the 1340s, to swords of different sizes and weights. A greater variety of pole-arms included the long-bladed gisarme with its thrusting point, the heavy poleaxe and the similar bill. There were also a few pikestaffs or pikes, as well as the halberd, halm barte, or shafted axe.

Cannon were used in small numbers in several parts of Europe by the 1340s. Ribaldis are first mentioned in the Privy Wardrobe accounts between February 1345 and March 1346, during preparations for the Crécy campaign. They would also appear in larger numbers at Edward III's siege of Calais in 1346-47, yet this ribald may still have been no more than a light cart. Only later in the 1380s would the ribaudekin clearly be a light or multiple gun mounted on cart-like wheels. Other cannon were, however, readied for the Crécy campaign. They are believed to have shot large arrows as well as cannon balls and perhaps a simple form of grapeshot. Limited as their effectiveness may have been, guns and gunpowder were so valuable that they were virtually confined to the Royal Wardrobe.

Another major concern for governments during the mid-14th century was the supply of horses of suitable quality. During the Sluys campaign of 1339 it was assumed that a man-at-arms needed three horses, a knight four, and a banneret five. They ranged from the very expensive destrier to the less costly courser and the cheapest equus, with huge price differentials within each category. The high wastage of horses on campaign meant that studs and breeding centres were vital, as was importation. The English government similarly banned the export of horses in times of crisis.

THE FRENCH

In France the old *service debitum* feudal system of military recruitment via the *ban* or *arrière ban*, a general levy, had virtually collapsed by the start of the 14th century when many troops won the right not to serve outside their own regions. During the early part of the 14th century, however, military obligations were extended to rear or secondary vassals, and in 1317 King Philip V reorganised the French army on this basis. Each town and castellany was responsible for providing a specified number of fully equipped troops, usually sergeants and infantry, while towns in economically advanced areas like Flanders became a major source of men and money. At the same time the old arrière ban was generally commuted in favour of taxation.

The aristocracy continued to form the basis of French armies. The aristocracy, the noblesse or chevalerie, differed from that of England in significant respects. It had become a hereditary caste whose members claimed privileges in taxation and law, as well as status and military rank, while the major provincial barons remained almost autonomous rulers within their own regions. There were between 45,000 and 50,000 noble families in the country, although those at the lower end of the scale could only afford the rank of squire. This meant that 2,350 to 4,000 fighting men, theoretically capable of serving as a man-at-arms, should have been available – four times as many as in England.

Philip VI abandoned traditional feudal vassal recruitment by 1350, except where a form of feudal annuity called the *fief-rente* was concerned. Here a man received payment in return for feudal military service and although this very expensive system was in decline by the mid-14th century, it played a significant role during the Crécy campaign. Hiring

The Church of St Saveur and, beyond it, the Abbaye aux Hommes in Caen. The spot where St Saveur now stands would have been inside the walls of the Old City in 1346, while the Abbaye stood outside. The English approached from the hills in the distance. (Author's photograph)

The 12th-13th-century walls of Caen castle on the northern side of the city were strong enough to defy the English conquerors. After Edward III moved on, the garrison emerged to destroy the small unit he left behind. (Author's photograph)

troops by verbal or written contract was becoming more important. The fully developed indenture system with a retaining fee, as seen in England, was rarely seen in France. Instead, military units simply left in search of other employers at the end of their contract, while failure to find such employment led to widespread banditry.

Philip VI and his successors also tried to develop a new form of feudal recruitment for men-at-arms, supplementing the now inadequate *ban* and *arrière ban*. The latter had demanded military service from all male subjects between the ages of 14 and 60, but the new semonce des nobles was directed towards all members of the nobility between those ages. Those summoned on this basis received daily wages similar to troops hired by contract. As a result French rulers were rarely short of fighting men. What they lacked were disciplined, trained and experienced soldiers. Another form of recruitment was the *arrière-ban aprés bataille*, or general call to arms after a major defeat, which implied a distinction between ordinary and crisis situations. In rural areas cart or wagon service provided the army with its transport. One example survives in a judgement of the Parlement de Paris, made on 2 June 1346. Apparently the villagers of Villeneuve-Saint-Georges had refused to provide wagon service to the local abbey in time of war because the claim of the Crown to such service was more important.

As in England, changes in recruitment made little difference to the composition or appearance of French armies. These forces were, however, large and expensive. The king's own contingent or hôtel generally cost less than one-tenth of the total, though the royal hôtel did include garrisons as well as the artillery train. Military expenditure also covered food, wine, fodder and wages. As a result Philip VI was almost constantly in financial difficulty, largely because France lacked a national system of approving taxation. The king had tried to solve this by first summoning the *arrière ban*, then commuting it for money. But the *arrière ban* could only be called after a war began, so forward military planning was virtually impossible. In 1345, during the build-up to the

Scene from *the Life of St. Nicholas* on a panel painting by Ambroglio Lorenzetti, *c.*1332 AD. The importance of this little picture lies in the fact that Lorenzetti showed the typical mid-14th century Italian great galleys with great accuracy, though the figures are out of scale. Such vessels would have formed part of the Genoese fleet which arrived in Normandy early in August 1346. (Uffizi Gallery, Florence)

Crécy campaign, Philip VI tried a new method of raising cash, with each locality paying a specified sum to furnish a specified number of sergeants or men-at-arms, and this proved quite effective. Defeats lowered royal prestige, however, which made it harder to gather taxes and raise new armies. In fact defeat fed upon defeat.

Following the military reorganisation of 1317, leaders and regional commanders were appointed directly by the crown. Of all the senior officers, the master of crossbowmen was the most strictly military, since other officers including the constable and the marshals also had political roles. Men supervising military expenditure in the king's own hôtel were also active soldiers, Philip VI's butler, Gille de Soyecourt, being killed at Crécy. The terms lance and glaive described a mounted man-at-arms with his squire and other support personnel, while infantry were generally grouped into constabularies or connétables. These usually

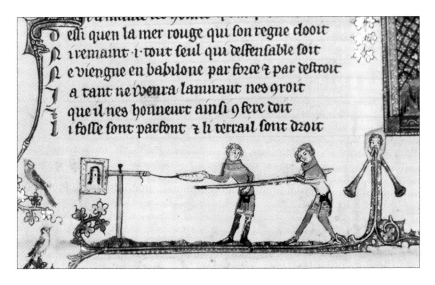

eſſi quen la mer rouge qui ſon regne clooit
i remaint i tout ſeul qui deſſenſable ſoit
e viengne en babilone par force z par deſtroit
a tant ne venra lamiraut nes groit
que il nes honneurt ainſi q fere doit
i foſſe ſont parfont z li terrail ſont droit

Youngsters train in the use of the lance, one boy charging towards a quintain that the second boy swings on a rope, as shown in the margin of a mid-14th-century Flemish manuscript. (*Romance of Alexander*, Bodleian Library, Ms. Bod. 246, f.82v, Oxford)

numbered from 45 to 55 men, although they could range between 20 and 150. Urban militiamen aged from 15 to 60 were often formed into dizaines, four of which formed a connétablie of about 100 men. As in England, the monarchy encouraged a revival of the chivalric ethos with its loyalty focused upon the Crown, resulting in the creation of the Order of the Star. Defeats during the early years of the war may also have encouraged all levels of society to group themselves around patrons for mutual support. This, however, fragmented the aristocracy into competing factions.

French defeats have given the impression that French commanders were outclassed by their supposedly more advanced English opponents. In fact, both sides faced similar constraints. The existing communications and transport systems meant that defence had to be organised locally, with small military units watching extensive frontiers, coasts and roads. It therefore seems remarkable that so little effort was put into improving French fortifications during the first decades of the war. In the prosperous but vulnerable north, several generations of relative peace had produced towns and even cities with few, inadequate or poorly maintained defences. In the generally flat or rolling countryside of northern France, walled towns were also militarily more important than in the rugged south. Here, major centres might have royal garrisons, but they were responsible for defending the entire area, not merely the town. At the same time the vital plat pays, the agricultural zone associated with a town or city, was more vulnerable in the north than the south. When danger did threaten an inadequately fortified town, the first priority was to strengthen walls and gates, organise guards, prohibit the export of foodstuffs, check the identity of strangers and get an exemption from sending troops to the arrière ban. The command structure and duties of each citizen had supposedly been arranged in advance, with the local militia being divided into squads of 10 to 50 men.

Until the end of the 13th century France had virtually no naval tradition along its Channel and Atlantic coasts, all previous naval emphasis having been in the Mediterranean. The Clos des Galées at Rouen, established in 1293, was the first arsenal in northern Europe. Like the galleys themselves, it was of Genoese design. Timber came from

A mid-14th-century fully armoured crossbowman on a carved altar from what is now eastern France. Many of the mercenary or allied infantry in Philip VI's army would have been equipped in this manner. (Church of St Nicholas, Hagenau; author's photograph)

the Cotentin peninsula, most of the shipbuilders and naval crews originated in Narbonne or Provence, while their officers were Genoese. In 1330 the Clos des Galées also started building northern ships, notably the Norman barge, which was a development of the old Scandinavian single-masted longship with the addition of fighting castles and a crew of 100 to 200 men. As in England, transport vessels were requisitioned when required. Scottish privateers were also welcomed in French ports as allies against their common English foe, many ships operating with mixed French and Scottish crews. Coastal defences were based upon a similar system to that in southern England. Even major coastal ports were virtually unfortified, but several small garrisons were supported by mobile forces based in three coastal zones, each under a 'captain of the sea frontier'. One stretched from the Flemish border to the Somme estuary; the next from the Somme to the Seine and the third from the Seine to the Breton border. Another covered the Atlantic coast from Brittany to English-ruled Gascony. Local militias and lordships supposedly reinforced the captains of the sea frontier, but usually arrived too late to be much help.

In battle the French still relied primarily upon the impact on morale of a fully-armoured cavalry charge in which men-at-arms operated in eschielles, or squadrons, which probably averaged around 100 horsemen. In such a charge it was normal to ride with a loose rein with the horses very close together. Banners still played a vital role, enabling cavalry and infantry to maintain cohesion and for men to rally around if they became separated; the fall of a banner was normally accepted as a time to retreat. It was now also usual for commanders to retain a cavalry reserve to take advantage of any break in the enemy line. At the battle of Crécy the impact of cavalry charges was intended to strike at morale rather than cause physical damage, but the impact on morale of French armoured cavalry had already failed against infantry in solid ranks several times before the outbreak of the Hundred Years War. Disciplined infantry armed with crossbows had similarly foiled cavalry charges in Italy and in the Iberian peninsula. What English infantry now brought to the battlefield was a massed use of longbows which proved even more effective in shattering the morale of armoured cavalry troops.

A crossbow was held laterally and could not be used in such close ranks as the hand bow, but the weight and superior aerodynamics of a crossbow bolt gave it greater penetrating power. The use of large numbers of crossbowmen in open battle also required close co-operation between crossbowmen, the pavesari, or shield-bearers behind whom up to three crossbowmen took turns to load, advance, shoot and retire, and the cavalry who defended their vulnerable flanks. Unfortunately problems of co-ordinating the actions of cavalry and infantry in early-14th-century French armies had led to the establishment of separate chains of command. It would be wrong to assume that French commanders were unable to learn from previous cavalry failures, but the

An Arthurian knight or man-at-arms armed in typical French equipment as illustrated in a French manuscript from around the time of Crécy. His horse is, however, completely unprotected. (*King Nabor and Sir Gawain*, Ms. Fr. 122, f. 80v, Bibliothèque Nationale, Ms. Fr. 122, f.80v, Paris)

A late-14th-century Italian infantry pavise, complete with the arms of Florence (among others). Such pavises provided protection for crossbowmen, and the Genoese lack of them at the battle of Crécy proved disastrous. (Private collection, Florence)

first recorded occasion when French men-at-arms dismounted to fight 'in the English manner' was less than three months before Crécy.

The military effectiveness of the French nobility was, in fact, in decline. The nobility had become a closed caste entered only by birth. The increasing cost of maintaining a noble lifestyle meant that many families entered trade and consequently the militarily active aristocracy was shrinking. Some families solved the problem by offering allegiance to more powerful noblemen in return for patronage. Others entered the direct service of king or Church, while in peaceful and prosperous Normandy the local knightly class had been virtually demilitarised for 100 years. Those of the senior French chevalerie who remained militarily active often regarded the primary role of knighthood as the achievement of personal or family honour through highly visible individual acts of prowess. This was fine during tournaments, but if it spilled over into battle the results could be disastrous, as at Crécy. The majority of French men-at-arms also tried to follow a knightly code known as the 'Law of Arms', which reduced the brutality of warfare, at least where fellow members of the aristocracy were concerned. In this they were helped by varlets, or servants, who did the dirty work of robbing or pillaging to obtain food on campaign. Varlets were often recruited for their local knowledge and, in 1351, appear to have been paid half as much as a squire. Aristocratic men-at-arms were similarly protected from the consequences of capture; their tenants were expected to pay ransoms since it was not in the government's interest that a noble family became destitute.

Many mid-14th-century French men-at-arms had wide military experience, ranging from the relatively humane battlefields of Italy to the rougher circumstances of Balkan, Mediterranean, Iberian and Baltic crusades. The large numbers of French soldiers who served as mercenaries in Italy must have learned the effectiveness of disciplined crossbow-armed infantry. Combat skills were taken similarly seriously by French men-at-arms. Training manuals had been known since at least the late-13th-century, and the attitudes expressed in such manuals are closer to those of modern commando training than the gentlemanly skills of a duel. When using a sword the thrust was already extolled over the cut, the main blows being aimed at an opponent's head. Physical fitness, agility and an ability to dodge or parry blows were all expected of a fully trained man-at-arms, who also trained hard to improve his horsemanship, particularly the ability to remount quickly in the press of battle.

Most French militia and mercenary infantry came under the authority of the Grand Master of Crossbowmen. Though larger towns employed professional guards and sergeants, and some had royal garrisons, their defence relied primarily on local militias. Many members of the aristocracy now lived in towns and although they would not normally serve in the guet or night watch on the ramparts, nor in guard daytime sentry duty at the gates, they probably assumed a command or leadership role. Urban knights may also have formed part of an arrière guet, or mounted reserve, within the walls. In France urban militias were obliged to send men to the king's muster who were normally dispersed among existing divisions when they reached the royal army. Militia crossbowmen would probably have been from slightly better-off backgrounds, as they were in Italy, and agreed to train regularly in exchange for certain tax exemptions.

The equipment of well-armed infantry in an army sent by Charles of Navarre to Normandy in 1357 consisted of lorigones (mail hauberks), bascinet helmets, plates or coats-of-plates armour, large pavois and smaller tablachos shields, plus crossbows. Among ordinary militiamen the poorest did not possess crossbows, the next grade had merely a crossbow, the next a crossbow and armour, while the top category was expected to provide arms for eight or so sergeants. Large-scale production of complex weapons like crossbows required sophisticated economic organisation, which could only be found in towns or cities. Many different craftsmen would be involved, all working in a co-ordinated manner. The resulting weapon required little strength and limited training to be effective, but confident teamwork between cross-bowmen and their supporting shield-bearers enabled a trained unit of crossbowmen to maintain a much faster rate of shooting than might be expected. Uniforms were rare, although one unit of royal crossbowmen had been issued with standard black cottes, or tunics, earlier in the 14th century. Discipline was severe, with the houses of militia deserters being pulled down. Other foot soldiers in mid-14th-century France included so-called brigans, brijantes or brigands. Some were relatively well armoured, although a similar term had previously been used in Italy and Savoy for low-status foot soldiers without crossbows. Later in the 14th century, of course, the word brigand came to mean a desperate robber, in many cases a recently demobilised soldier.

Most of those units which were called companies stemmed from, or were formed by the lords of regions closely associated with France. During the early decades of the Hundred Years War companies of men-at-arms came from neighbouring parts of the German Empire such as Liège, Cologne, Guelders, Juliers and more distant Bavaria. Some units were small, less than 100 men, and as the years passed they became smaller still. Bohemia was also part of the Empire and some of its knights are believed to have followed John of Luxembourg, King of Bohemia, to Crécy. Bohemia was, however, a relatively backward part of central Europe where arms and armour seem to have been old fashioned.

France's weakness in archery was recognised well before Crécy. In 1336 King Philip recruited crossbowmen in Brabant in what is now Belgium. In 1345 he tried to do the same in Aragon, while Provence in south-eastern France was another significant source. Italy remained the main reservoir of qualified crossbowmen. It was the most densely populated part of medieval Europe and practice with the weapon was an obligation for men throughout much of the country, so there were many

a Seal of Charles II de Valois, Count of Alençon, 1329-46. (Cabinet des Médailles aux Archives Nationales, Paris)

b Seal of Carlo Grimaldi II Grande, first ruler of autonomous Monaco, 1341-57. (after E. E. Robella)

c Seal of Raoul, Duke of Lorraine, 1329-46, dated February 1334. (Archives du Meurthe and Moselle, Nancy)

d Seal of John of Luxembourg, king of Bohemia, also showing him as ruler of Poland, 1310-46, dated 1314. (Staatsarchivs, no. 2729, Or. Reg. Luxembourg, Berlin)

qualified crossbowmen available. Italian crossbowmen had, in fact, served France since at least the early-14th century. The most famous were the so-called Genoese, who actually came from many different places, even beyond Italy. To describe them as mercenaries is misleading since Genoa was an ally of France. In fact many of these crossbowmen, their pavesarii (shield-bearers), the fleet in which they served and the men who recruited them, had long experience of serving France.

Italians had long dominated trade and warfare in the Mediterranean and they were now a force to be reckoned with in the Atlantic. Their galleys carried large fighting crews and their marines also fought on land, presumably using light ballistae crossbows rather than the heavy weapons also carried by many galleys. In 1340, for example, a large Genoese galley in French service carried 40 ballistae, normally with around 100 quarrels, or arrows, for each. According to Clos des Galées records for 1346-47, the master of a galley called the Sainte Marie was Crestien di Grimault (or Grimaldi), with a crew of 210 men, consisting of one comite, one souz comite, one clerk, one under-clerk and 205 crossbowmen and sailors plus the master. This ship left Nice on 24 May 1346 and was contracted to serve for 161 days at 900 gold florins per month, plus 30 florins per extra day.

It is not clear how such men were organised when serving on land, but presumably those from one ship would remain together. Records from late-13th-century Venice mention naval spears or pikes, 5 metres long with shafts of ash or beech. Since there were usually more than three crossbowmen for each shield-bearer, it would seem that these crossbowmen took turns to shoot from behind cover provided by the shield-bearer, then stepped back to span and load their weapon before returning to shoot. If this was their normal tactic, then the Genoese

The Seine valley near Elbeuf. Here Edward III had to decide whether to attack Rouen, attack Paris, cross the River Seine and join his Flemish allies, or return the way he had come. It is still one of the richest and most fertile parts of northern France. The Seine was also a vital strategic and trade link between Paris and the sea. (Author's photograph)

failure at Crécy becomes easier to understand, since here they were operating without their mantlet-shields. Quite what the pavesarii (shield-bearers) were expected to do when the Genoese infantry were ordered forward at Crécy is unknown, though written sources mention spearmen advancing with the crossbowmen. Such teams of soldiers were essentially static or defensive troops and the decision to send them forward against the English at Crécy may indicate that the French commanders had little idea how to use what were at that time regarded as the finest infantry in Christian Europe.

King Philip VI took a close interest in the theoretical aspects of warfare, offering his patronage to Guido da Vigevano, the author of the 1335 *Texaurus*. This book was intended as a source of military advice for a future Crusade and 14 of its 23 sections are devoted to military technology. The *Texaurus* is also more original and practical than other military treatise written in the period. Most of its technical terms are in Italian, not Latin, and reflect the flourishing technology of an age when Latin could no longer cope with the language of real machine developments.

Of more immediate concern, however, was the manufacture and purchase of large quantities of arms and armour. Such equipment took a long time to manufacture but was easy to store. Consequently arms and armour merchants built up their stocks in time of peace, ready to sell them in time of crisis. Italian merchants seem to have dominated this trade, Italy producing the finest armour, and Germany manufacturing the best blades. France, like England, also had its own arms manufacturing centres. By the 1330s and 1340s the Clos des Galées, for example, was turning out huge quantities of couteaux (daggers), lances, dards (javelins), haches norroises (axes), as well as crossbows, garrocs to span crossbows, crossbow stirrups, quarrels (arrows) and 'spinning' viretons. In 1340 it had no less than 3,000 to 4,000 crossbows, tens of thousands of quarrels, as well as spears, javelins and other weapons in store. Viretons were manufactured in hundreds of thousands. The average cost of a crossbow was quite cheap at 11 sous and 5 deniers, most having bows of composite construction, which, though coated with another substance, were vulnerable to damp. The standard war crossbow would have been spanned using a belt and hook, possibly incorporating a pulley, with straps and belts to suit the size and strength of the man.

Other French weapons were the same as those used by their English opponents, though French infantry may have made greater use of the barde, a long-hafted axe with a thrusting point. Both the French and the Genoese may similarly have used the tavelas, a large round or oval infantry shield. Since the French were on the defensive during the Crécy campaign, they made more use of static siege weaponry. Written records indicate that the stores of a walled town or castle anticipating a siege should include timber, lime, stones, bricks, tiles, nails, pitch, tar, rope, canvas thread, hide, leather, coal, iron, lead, saltpetre, carts, cord, ammunition for springalds (frame-mounted weapons comparable to very large crossbows), crossbows, armour and weapons, plus boats and naval tackle for coastal or riverside locations. The French were, in fact, ahead of the English when it came to firearms. One French ship used a gun at sea in 1338, and cannon helped save Cambrai from Anglo-Flemish hands the following year.

THE OPPOSING PLANS

THE ENGLISH INVASION PLAN

Six-and-a-half centuries after the event, Edward III's original intentions remain unknown, although a grand strategy whereby several armies converged on Paris from Normandy, Flanders, Brittany and Gascony is extremely unlikely. Perhaps Edward hoped to conquer the northern coastal regions, then add them to Brittany where his allies were doing well. If so, the plan proved impossible and Edward's campaign became little more than a great chevauchée, or raid. On the other hand all major English campaigns from 1344 to 1359, including that of Crécy, may simply have been political demonstrations to lay bare Philip VI's weakness. Edward's military 'might' would thus strengthen his 'right' to the French Crown.

It has been suggested that after Edward's fleet sailed home laden with booty following the fall of Caen, he had no choice but to march overland towards the supplies he hoped to find at Le Crotoy in Ponthieu. It is unlikely that Edward III wanted a major battle with Philip until after he had linked up with the Flemings, so their retreat would have come as unpleasant news. Once a battle became inevitable, however, Edward III's plans made it clear that he wanted to fight the French cavalry rather than their infantry. Consequently, he provoked cavalry charges uphill against obstacles defended by well-prepared infantry formations. Once the Genoese had been defeated, this was of course precisely what happened.

THE FRENCH DEFENCE PLAN

Philip VI had almost no choice but to adopt a defensive strategy in which local forces tried to defend towns in the English path and harassed the invaders while the king assembled an army to face them openly. If it became impossible for the English to administer the territory they had conquered, then in time the French could retake it. In fact this is what happened in Normandy. Only at Calais were the invaders determined to hold what they overran. After Edward III's army crossed the River Seine, Philip VI may have hoped that by vigorously pursuing the English he could encourage them to leave France without a major battle. This hope was shattered when he came upon the English army in a well-prepared position at Crécy.

Once a major battle became inevitable, Philip's previous experience may have misled him. At Cassel in 1328 a well-judged French cavalry attack against the Flemish flank had brought rapid victory. King Philip's other successes at Buironfosse in 1339 and Bouvines in 1340 had been 'non-battles' where a patient avoidance of combat had defeated two of Edward III's previous campaigns. But such tactics required a strong political position. Following the devastation caused by the English since landing in Normandy, not to mention the taunts of those who described this as the 'behaviour of the fox and not the lion', King Philip was under pressure to act decisively.

THE CAMPAIGN

THE INVASION

The English army which assembled around Portsmouth in May and June 1346 was very large, though not as large as Edward III had hoped. The mustering was also slower than intended. Nevertheless, King Edward took the risk of exposing the country to Scottish raids by recruiting everywhere except in the most northerly counties. At least half the army seem to have been archers, but it included miners, masons, smiths, farriers, engineers, carpenters, tent-makers, surgeons, officials, clerks and the men-at-arms.

The resulting force numbered between 10,000 and 15,000 and required at least 750 ships. The gathering of this fleet was similarly delayed by storms. The largest vessels were 200-ton cogs, but a shortage of suitable ships meant that 10-ton craft were requisitioned, perhaps including the coastal ships which brought huge amounts of food to the assembly point. Edward III himself arrived at Porchester Castle on 1 June to supervise operations, while the government used various forms of propaganda to whip up anti-French feeling. Troops were then paid an extra fortnight's wages in advance, and the ports of London, Dover, Winchelsea and Sandwich were closed to prevent news of the invasion fleet reaching France. No ships were allowed to leave until a week after the fleet had sailed, the only exception being Sir Hugh Hastings and the men he was taking to Flanders.

Quite when Edward III changed his final plans is unclear, but it may have been during a secret meeting around 20 June. It had previously been assumed that the fleet would sail to Gascony and the ships were victualled for a two-week journey. But then Edward III either changed his mind or told his commanders his true plans, which were to land on the Cotentin peninsula of Normandy.

Another invasion would be launched from Flanders, supported by Sir Hugh Hastings, a knight from Norfolk with a small force of 18 barges, 250 archers and some men-at-arms. On 24 June the leaders of Ghent, Bruges and Ypres had accepted English direction and on 16 July Hastings left for Ghent, where Flemish forces were assembling under the nominal command of Count Henry of Flanders. The neighbouring rulers of Brabant and Hainault had meanwhile agreed to support Philip VI of France, counter-balancing Edward's Flemish alliance.

The French knew that invasions were imminent but they were severely hampered by not knowing the destination of the English fleet. Defence preparations had been under way since 18 March, with Brittany or Gascony as the anticipated targets. Charles of Blois recruited widely in Brittany and enlisted foreign troops, while in May Philip VI sent reinforcements drawn from the Duke of Normandy's army in Gascony.

This left a few scattered garrisons and some Genoese crossbowmen in Normandy and Picardy, where a state of emergency was declared with

An early-14th-century French or Italian bronze aquamanile, an elaborate wine or water dispenser, in the form of a fully armoured knight. (Bargello Museum, Florence)

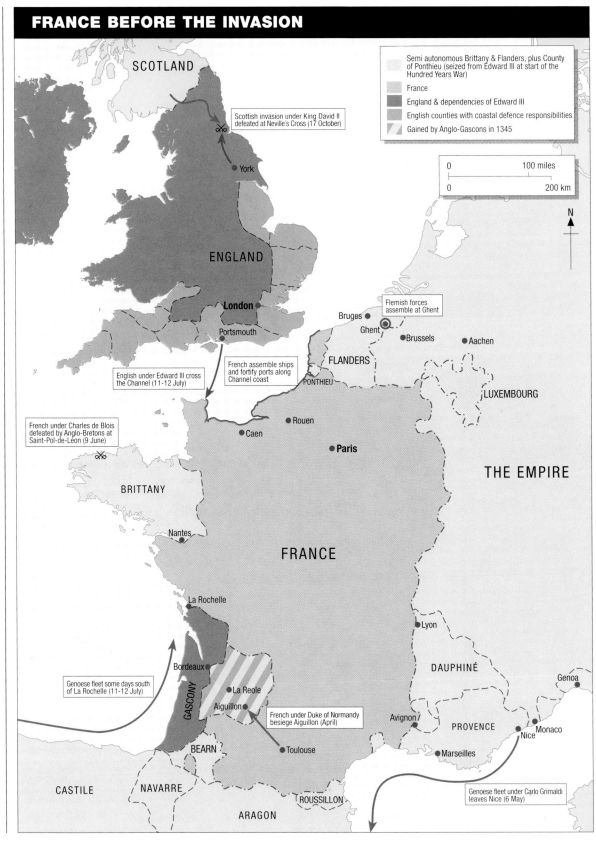

SCOTLAND

Scottish invasion under King David II
defeated at Neville's Cross (17 October)

York

ENGLAND

London

Portsmouth

Flemish forces
assemble at Ghent

Bruges

Ghent

Brussels

Aachen

FLANDERS

English under Edward III cross
the Channel (11-12 July)

French assemble ships
and fortify ports along
Channel coast

PONTHIEU

LUXEMBOURG

French under Charles de Blois
defeated by Anglo-Bretons at
Saint-Pol-de-Léon (9 June)

Rouen

Caen

Paris

THE EMPIRE

BRITTANY

Nantes

FRANCE

La Rochelle

Lyon

Genoese fleet some days south
of La Rochelle (11-12 July)

Bordeaux

GASCONY

La Reole

Aiguillon

French under Duke of Normandy
besiege Aiguillon (April)

DAUPHINÉ

Genoa

Avignon

PROVENCE

Nice

Monaco

BEARN

Toulouse

Marseilles

CASTILE

NAVARRE

ROUSSILLON

Genoese fleet under Carlo Grimaldi
leaves Nice (6 May)

ARAGON

N

0	100 miles
0	200 km

Semi autonomous Brittany & Flanders, plus County
of Ponthieu (seized from Edward III at start of the
Hundred Years War)

France

England & dependencies of Edward III

English counties with coastal defence responsibilities

Gained by Anglo-Gascons in 1345

One of the smaller wall-paintings in Avio Castle shows cross-bowmen and pavesarii operating together. It dates from around 1360. (Castle of Sabbionara, Avio; author's photograph)

crude attempts to block harbours with wooden piles. Apparently King Philip hoped to intercept the English at sea and a census of available shipping was made. At least 78 larger ships were requisitioned and fitted with wooden castles in Lower Normandy, with more in Upper Normandy and Picardy. Genoese officers and crossbowmen were placed aboard to serve as auxiliaries for a substantial force of Genoese war galleys. Unfortunately the Genoese galley fleet was delayed and only arrived in August. Their advance guard had left Nice under the command of Carlo Grimaldi on 6 May, as it was not possible to cross the Bay of Biscay any earlier. They were then scattered by an Atlantic storm and took refuge in the Tagus estuary in Portugal, where they remained in early July.

Back in France, Charles of Blois had launched a major offensive in Brittany but had suffered a severe setback at Saint-Pol de Leon on 9 June. In Gascony the Duke of Normandy was making no progress in his siege of English-held Aiguillon. A direct assault had failed, the French besiegers were short of food and their widely spread foragers were harassed by forces sympathetic to the English. Then, late in June Philip VI realised that the main threat was in the north and recalled the Constable of France with part of the Duke of Normandy's army. He was placed in command of Harfleur on the Seine estuary and the Count of Flanders was sent to join him. The Marshals of France were probably also recalled from the south, precautions were stepped up along the Channel coast and summonses were sent to recruit a northern army. The Scots did not break their truce with England, but massed along the border once Edward had broken his truce with France. The urgency of Philip's letter to King David of Scotland in June is obvious: 'I beg you, I implore you with all the force that I can, to remember the bonds of blood and friendship between us. Do for me what I would willingly do for you in such a crisis, and do it as quickly and as thoroughly as with God's help you are able.'

Edward III boarded ship on 28 June and, after several days of contrary winds, sailed to Yarmouth on the Isle of Wight where he waited for the rest of the fleet. Unfavourable winds then forced the whole

This well-known English marginal illumination made around 1340 shows archers practising at the butts. Their blunt-tipped arrows were not the sort used in warfare and the men are, of course, unarmoured. (*Luttrell Psalter*, British Library, Ms. Add. 42130, f. 147v, London)

armada back to Portsmouth and Forland. On 3 July Edward III again sailed to Yarmouth to be followed by the rest of the fleet until ships were anchored as far as the Needles. Again the wind veered, making this anchorage unsafe, so they returned to Portsmouth harbour for a further nine or ten days. Finally, on 11 July the armada broke free and, with perfect wind and tides, assembled off St Helens. There Edward III gave sealed orders to his captains before almost 1,000 assorted vessels set off for Normandy. They arrived before dawn on the 12th and anchored off a broad beach at Saint-Marco outside Saint-Vaast-la-Hogue. The Genoese fleet, which had been sent to intercept them, was still several days south of La Rochelle, and French ships were beached in various harbours awaiting them. Fourteen were at Saint-Vaast, and the eight most heavily armed were burned by the invaders. Wooden stakes blocking the harbour caused no serious problems to the invaders, and the abandoned town was sacked.

The main French forces were north of the Seine, leaving Marshal Robert Bertrand, captain of the sea frontier, with very few troops. He had, however, been planning to inspect the Saint-Vaast militia on the day the English arrived. So Bertrand assembled around 300 poorly trained locals and made a brief, unsuccessful counter-attack that morning. But the English already had several thousand men ashore, so Bertrand retreated south with his own retainers, gathering other local forces as he went.

Around midday King Edward landed and, according to Froissart, tripped with his first step on to the beach. Some regarded this as a bad omen but Edward III supposedly replied, 'Why? I look upon it as very favourable for me, as a sign that the land desires to have me.' The king then knighted some young noblemen to mark their first active service, including his son Edward, Prince of Wales. Next, the royal party climbed a hill to survey the area. Godfrey de Harcourt and the Earl of Warwick were appointed as the army's two marshals, with the Earl of Arundel as its constable. The Earl of Huntingdon was put in command of the fighting ships with 100 men-at-arms and 400 archers.

From 13 to 17 July the English disembarked men and supplies while raiding the surrounding territory. On the 14th Barfleur was assaulted from land and sea. It surrendered and some leading citizens were taken for ransom while the town was pillaged then burned, as were nine warships in the harbour. The booty included gold, silver, jewels and, according to Froissart, 'There was so much wealth that even the servants of the army set no value upon gowns trimmed with fur.' The raiders then burned the Abbey of Nôtre Dame du Voeu in Cherbourg, although they were unable to take the town's castle. In fact an area 35 kilometres around the landing point was devastated, its inhabitants fleeing into the woods or trekking south as refugees.

The English army was now divided into three divisions. One followed the coast, one under Edward III remained in the centre, while the third followed a road further inland. The Earl of Northampton now seems to have been made constable and Edward III ordered that there should be no further destruction of life or property, though this had no effect on the behaviour of his troops. Most of the ships were sent home, but 200 larger vessels sailed along the coast, destroying or capturing every ship they found and devastating an eight kilometre-wide belt to undermine the basis of French naval power.

Fully armoured knights in combat in a mid-14th-century Flemish manuscript. The lack of visors may simply enable the artist to show their faces. All the horses have chamfrons to protect their heads, while that of the king also has a full heraldic caparison. (*Romance of Alexander*, Bodleian Library, Ms. Bod. 246, Oxford)

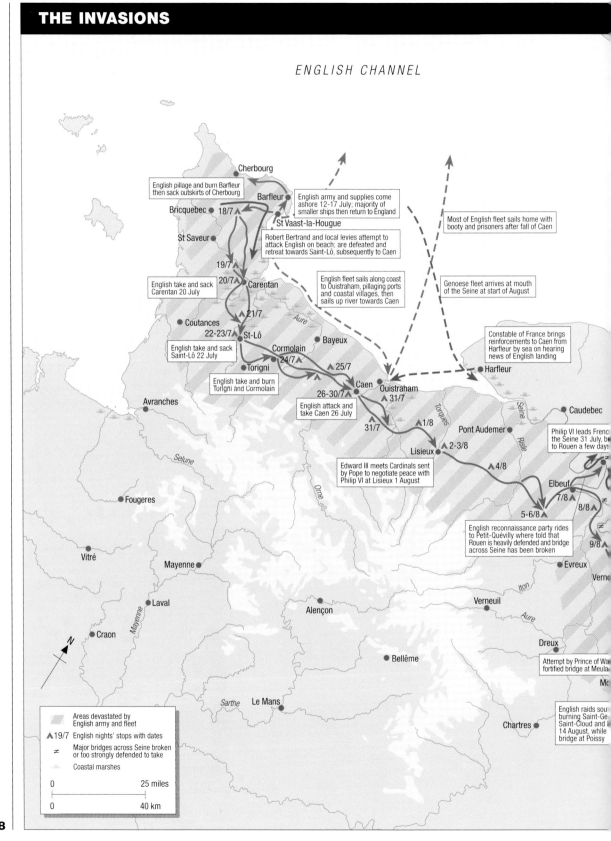

ENGLISH CHANNEL

Cherbourg

English pillage and burn Barfleur
then sack outskirts of Cherbourg

Barfleur

Bricquebec ● 18/7
St Vaast-la-Hougue

English army and supplies come
ashore 12-17 July; majority of
smaller ships then return to England

St Saveur ●

Robert Bertrand and local levies attempt to
attack English on beach; are defeated and
retreat towards Saint-Lô, subsequently to Caen

Most of English fleet sails home with
booty and prisoners after fall of Caen

19/7

20/7
Carentan

English take and sack
Carentan 20 July

English fleet sails along coast
to Ouistraham, pillaging ports
and coastal villages, then
sails up river towards Caen

Genoese fleet arrives at mouth
of the Seine at start of August

21/7
Aure

Coutances ●
22-23/7
St-Lô

English take and sack
Saint-Lô 22 July

Cormolain
24/7

Bayeux

Constable of France brings
reinforcements to Caen from
Harfleur by sea on hearing
news of English landing

25/7

English take and burn
Turigni and Cormolain

Torigni ●

Harfleur ●

Avranches ●

26-30/7

Caen
Ouistraham
31/7

English attack and
take Caen 26 July

Seine

Caudebec ●

31/7

1/8
Torques

Pont Audemer ●

Philip VI leads Frenc[h]
the Seine 31 July, b[ut]
to Rouen a few days

Lisieux ●
2-3/8

Risle

Selune

Edward III meets Cardinals sent
by Pope to negotiate peace with
Philip VI at Lisieux 1 August

4/8

Elbeuf ●
7/8

8/8

Fougeres ●

5-6/8

9/8

Orne

English reconnaissance party rides
to Petit-Quévilly where told that
Rouen is heavily defended and bridge
across Seine has been broken

Evreux ●

Vern[...]

Vitré ●

Mayenne ●

Alençon ●

Verneuil ●

Iton

Mayenne

Laval ●

Aure

Dreux ●

Craon ●

N

Bellême ●

Attempt by Prince of Wa[les]
fortified bridge at Meula[n]

Mo[...]

Sarthe
Le Mans ●

English raids sou[...]
burning Saint-Ge[...]
Saint-Cloud and [...]
14 August, while [...]
bridge at Poissy

Chartres ●

Areas devastated by
English army and fleet

▲19/7 English nights' stops with dates

≉ Major bridges across Seine broken
or too strongly defended to take

Coastal marshes

0   25 miles

0   40 km

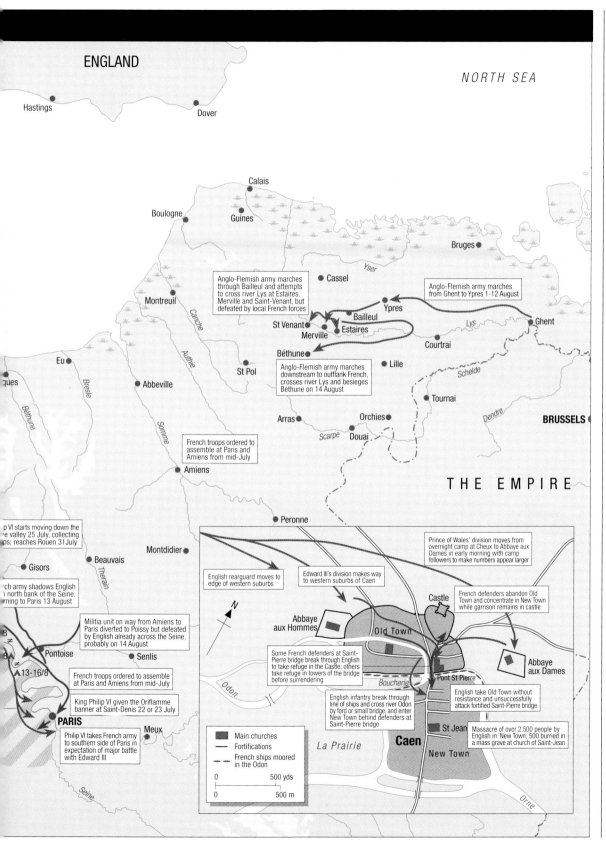

ENGLAND

NORTH SEA

Hastings

Dover

Calais

Boulogne

Guines

Bruges

Yser

Cassel

Montreuil

Ypres

Anglo-Flemish army marches
through Bailleul and attempts
to cross river Lys at Estaires,
Merville and Saint-Venant, but
defeated by local French forces

Anglo-Flemish army marches
from Ghent to Ypres 1-12 August

St Venant Bailleul

Merville Estaires

Lys Ghent

Canche

Courtrai

Béthune

Lille

Anglo-Flemish army marches
downstream to outflank French,
crosses river Lys and besieges
Béthune on 14 August

Eu

St Pol

Tournai

Schelde

Authie

ques

Abbeville

Bresle

Béthune

Arras

Orchies

Dendre

BRUSSELS

Somme

Scarpe Douai

French troops ordered to
assemble at Paris and
Amiens from mid-July

Amiens

THE EMPIRE

Peronne

p VI starts moving down the
e valley 25 July, collecting
ps; reaches Rouen 31 July

Gisors

Montdidier

Beauvais

Therain

ch army shadows English
n north bank of the Seine,
rning to Paris 13 August

Prince of Wales' division moves from
overnight camp at Cheux to Abbaye aux
Dames in early morning with camp
followers to make numbers appear larger

English rearguard moves to
edge of western suburbs

Edward III's division makes way
to western suburbs of Caen

French defenders abandon Old
Town and concentrate in New Town
while garrison remains in castle

Castle

N

Militia unit on way from Amiens to
Paris diverted to Poissy but defeated
by English already across the Seine,
probably on 14 August

8

Pontoise

Senlis

Abbaye
aux Hommes

Old Town

13-16/8

French troops ordered to assemble
at Paris and Amiens from mid-July

Some French defenders at Saint-
Pierre bridge break through English
to take refuge in the Castle; others
take refuge in towers of the bridge
before surrendering

Boucherie

Pont St Pierre

English take Old Town without
resistance and unsuccessfully
attack fortified Saint-Pierre bridge

PARIS

Meux

King Philip VI given the Oriflamme
banner at Saint-Denis 22 or 23 July

English infantry break through
line of ships and cross river Odon
by ford or small bridge, and enter
New Town behind defenders at
Saint-Pierre bridge

Abbaye
aux Dames

Philip VI takes French army
to southern side of Paris in
expectation of major battle
with Edward III

Odon

St Jean

Massacre of over 2,500 people by
English in New Town; 500 burried in
a mass grave at church of Saint-Jean

Main churches

Fortifications

French ships moored
in the Odon

La Prairie

Caen

New Town

0   500 yds

0   500 m

Seine

Orne

39

ABOVE, LEFT **The subsidiary figures on the monumental brass of Sir Hugh Hastings include many leading English military commanders of the mid-14th century. It was made around 1347-48. This figure represents Thomas Beauchamp, third Earl of Warwick. (Elsing Church)**

ABOVE, RIGHT **A deed relating to a property transaction in Sussex, dated November 1341 and bearing, on the right, the seal of Richard Fitzalan, the third Earl of Arundel. (Archives, Arundel Castle)**

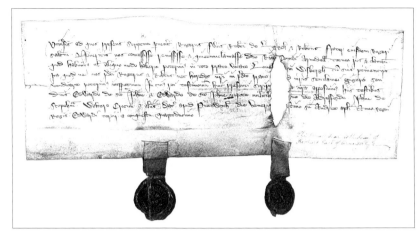

Chevauchée or Conquest?

By 18 July the disembarkation was finished, the horses rested, supplies organised and bread baked for the next few days, although the English still had to forage widely. Godfrey de Harcourt, whose family estates were at the southern end of the Cotentin peninsula, soon proved his value as one of the army's leading scouts. With an advance guard of 500 men-at-arms and 1,000 archers he marched 30 kilometres ahead and to the right of the king's division. The coastal division was regarded as a vanguard and, nominally led by the young Prince of Wales, was actually commanded by the earls of Northampton and Warwick. The inland division acted as the rearguard under Thomas Hatfield, Bishop of Durham.

The English finally left Saint-Vaast on 18 July, marching along narrow lanes to Valognes, where Edward III spent the night in a house owned by the Duke of Normandy. Next day the troops burned Montebourg before spending the next night divided between Saint-Côme-du-Mont and Coigny, where King Edward learned that the bridge over the Douve was broken. Since there was only a narrow impractical causeway across the neighbouring marshes, teams of carpenters spent the night repairing this bridge. The nearby town of Carentan was large and well stocked with supplies, much of which was destroyed when English soldiers set fire to the place. Resistance was brief, apparently because the garrison had been provided by Godfrey de Harcourt's men. They and perhaps some reinforcements were left in control when the English moved on, taking with them leading citizens for ransom.

Like several other places in the Cotentin peninsula, Carentan was soon retaken by French troops, its treacherous garrison being sent to Paris and executed. Otherwise, all that Marshal Robert Bertrand could do was harass the advancing English hordes while more effective resistance was prepared at Caen, where the Constable of France, Count Raoul II d'Eu, had transferred his available troops by boat from Harfleur. There were not enough men to garrison all the castles ahead of the English advance and only a few were defended as Robert Bertrand fell back.

The English, however, were delayed by broad marshes between Saint-Côme and Carentan, and between Saint-Lô and Bayeux, where several causeways had to be rebuilt. Bertrand had intended to defend Saint-Lô, but realised it was impossible once the English had rebuilt a bridge

The River Somme just east of Hengest-sur-Somme, between Amiens and Abbeville. All the bridges along this stretch of river were either broken or very strongly defended by the French, while fords such as that at Hengest would probably also have been closely watched. (Author's photograph)

across the Vire, so he abandoned the town to its fate. Edward III's division now had to wait almost three days outside Saint-Lô before the coastal division could reach him. The re-assembled army then put its booty into wagons before moving forward. This time the earls of Warwick and Suffolk, Lord Thomas Holland, Reginald Cobham and their division advanced on the left, burning and destroying, while the right under Godfrey de Harcourt did the same. Rumours that the French were massing around the Cistercian abbey at Torigny prompted the main English force to change direction towards Cormolain; the advance party, heading for Torigny, caught up later. Over the following two days Edward moved very cautiously, with the rearguard only reaching slightly beyond the advance guard's starting point of the previous morning. The head of the great army came in sight of the city of Caen on the evening of the 24th, while 200 ships which had followed the army along the coast, sailed up the River Orne to arrive around the same time. By this time the ships were so laden with plunder that they could not carry all the booty the army had won.

Caen stood in the middle of an open plain without natural defences. The city was split between the Old Town and the New Town, divided by the Odon stream. Its crumbling 11th-century fortifications consisted partly of wooden walls and partly of a stone wall with marshes on one

The effigy of Sir Richard de Goldsborough the Younger, dating from around 1340, is unusual because the sculptor shows the interior of his shield in detail. This includes the nails holding the enarmes straps and the thickly padded leather lining. The armour is, however, remarkably old-fashioned for the date. (Goldsborough Church; authors' photograph)

side. The only substantial fortification was a castle at the northern edge of town. Outside the city the Abbaye aux Dames and the Abbaye aux Hommes had defensive walls, but there were not enough men to garrison them. The defenders of Caen were now commanded by Raoul d'Eu, who also had a small unit of Genoese crossbowmen, some 800 Norman knights and men-at-arms, and the city militia, a total of around 4,000 men. Efforts had been made to strengthen the old walls with trenches and palisades, while 30 or so small ships manned by cross-bowmen were moored in the Odon between the Old and New towns.

Edward III had many more men, but he lacked heavy siege equipment and the French defenders refused to be intimidated, even throwing Edward's envoy, the friar Geoffrey of Maldon, into prison. At dawn on 26 July the Prince of Wales' division set fire to their overnight lodgings at Cheux and made their way around Caen to the Abbaye aux Dames. King Edward established his headquarters in the western suburbs while the English rearguard pitched its tents just beyond. When they saw the size of the English army, the French commanders decided to abandon the Old Town and concentrate their troops in the New Town, which, though it stood on the island of Saint-Jean, was now separated from the castle commanded by the Bishop of Bayeux. The people of Caen similarly concentrated in the New Town. Unfortunately, the towers of the fortified Pont Saint-Pierre were now on the wrong side of the river, so an improvised barricade was added to the northern side. Worse still, the River Odon was low during that notably dry summer.

Early in the morning the Old Town was apparently taken without resistance, and units under Warwick, Northampton and Talbot attacked the Pont Saint-Pierre without success. A group of English and Welsh infantry was therefore sent across the Odon some 200 metres away, either by a bridge at the Boucherie or via an undefended ford. But they still had to break through the line of ships: two were set on fire and the remainder retreated as the English entered the New Town. The defenders of the Pont Saint-Pierre were now surrounded. Some, including Robert Bertrand, fought their way to the castle; others, including the Count d'Eu, took refuge in the towers until they could surrender, but many were killed where they stood. Valuable prisoners were sent back to England with the Earl of Huntingdon, who had fallen ill. Massacre, rape and looting followed: over 2,500 inhabitants of Caen were killed, 500 of whom were tipped into a mass grave at the church of Saint-Jean.

The English then rested for five days while the surrounding countryside was systematically burned. On 29 July King Edward also sent a letter to the Council of England, ordering them to recruit men-at-arms and an additional 1,200 archers from areas not already emptied of fighting men, along with large quantities of munitions, money and 100 ships to bring the reinforcements to France. They were to land at Le Crotoy on the northern side of the Somme estuary in Ponthieu – territory which the English had yet to conquer.

The French Reaction
Philip VI of France probably got news of the invasion on 16 July and he spent the next fortnight organising a muster of troops at Paris and Amiens. On the 22nd or 23rd Philip went to the great church of Saint-Denis to receive the sacred Oriflamme banner, which was only used

The existing bridge over the Somme at Pont Remy is modern, while the church largely dates from the 19th century. Here a substantial English force under Godfrey de Harcourt tried to force a crossing but were defeated by John of Luxembourg's troops on the north bank. (Author's photograph)

The famous stained glass window in Tewkesbury Abbey was made around 1344. It includes a large number of military figures, including the earls of Gloucester and members of the Clare family. All have slightly different arms and armour. On the left is Gilbert de Clare I, and on the right William, Lord Zouche of Mortimer. (Abbey Church, Tewkesbury; author's photograph)

during the defence of France. On the 25th he set out down the Seine valley while troops assembled from all directions. He also sent another letter to King David of Scotland, whose men raided Cumberland late in July. But the Scots were not willing to commit themselves to a full-scale invasion and made a two-month truce with the lords of northern England. Philip VI hurried on to Rouen, as his primary concern was to stop Edward taking this city and blocking the Seine. The Genoese galley fleet also arrived early in August and, as it was too late to stop the invasion, the crews joined Philip's army as infantry. Meanwhile, the English were still at Lisieux and on the 31st Philip crossed the Seine and began moving cautiously towards them. On 2 August two cardinals, sent by the Pope to negotiate peace, are said to have reached the French camp.

About now Philip VI was warned of an imminent Flemish invasion and as there were only a handful of French garrisons close to the northern frontier, most of the militia and other units assembling at Amiens were held back to defend the line of the Somme. The Flemish invaders in fact set out on 1 August under the nominal authority of Count Henry of Flanders, although Sir Hugh Hastings was in actual command. On the 2nd they left Ypres and marched via Bailleul to the River Lys. Here there were minor clashes at Estaires, Merville and Saint-Venant before Hugh Hastings led the Flemish downstream to outflank the French defenders. Their march was still painfully slow but on 14 August they reached Béthune, which they besieged.

Quite how Edward III and the Flemish force communicated is unknown, but they undoubtedly did so. For his part Philip decided to defend the Seine rather than risk placing the river between himself and the new Flemish threat. His army returned to Rouen and all the bridges between Paris and the sea were broken or heavily defended. Towns south of the river were authorised to empty their prisons if they needed more defenders and more of the militia assembling at Amiens were ordered to join Philip.

As the English moved up the south bank of the Seine, there was near panic in Paris and John of Luxembourg was sent to keep control with 500 men-at-arms while the Paris militias prepared to defend the city. Edward III clearly had the initiative: Philip VI's army was still small, many of the Genoese were dispersed in garrisons and Philip was in danger of spreading his forces too thinly along the winding River Seine. Under these circumstances Philip decided to establish his headquarters at Saint-Denis while the bulk of his army camped nearby at Saint-Cloud. Far to the south the youthful Duke of Normandy still insisted on taking the stubborn castle of Aiguillon, at least until King Philip sent direct orders for him to march north; on 20 August the duke finally abandoned his camp and crossed the Garonne.

The English withdrew from Caen on 31 July, leaving behind a small force to blockade the castle. The French garrison soon took the offensive, however, and killed virtually all the English troops in Caen. Edward III marched to Troarn, Argences and Lisieux, which he entered on 1 August, and discovered the two cardinals who had been sent to make peace. Two days of negotiations came to nothing, although some of the unruly Welsh troops stole 20 horses from the cardinals' retinue.

In the light of Philip's preparation for a counter-attack the English now advanced with greater caution. They halted for a probable council of war on the 6th and next day changed direction towards Rouen, reaching the River Seine at Elbeuf. Edward may have hoped to find Rouen virtually undefended, but a reconnaissance under Godfrey de Harcourt discovered that the French army was already in the city and the Seine bridge was down. This was a setback and Edward now had to decide whether to race for Paris or to try to cross the river to link up with his Flemish allies in Picardy. The bridge at Pont de l'Arche proved too strongly defended to take and Philip VI was shadowing the English from the north bank. Nevertheless, the invaders devastated a strip of land over 30 kilometres wide south of the Seine. They burned Louviers and Gaillon, and unsuccessfully attacked a castle where Sir Richard Talbot and Sir Thomas Holland were both wounded. On the 9th the English also failed to seize Vernon. Next day a raiding party crossed the Seine and took La Roche-Guyon by assault, but this was not a suitable place for the whole army to cross.

At Freneuse the cardinals returned with Philip VI's final offer of peace terms, including a marriage alliance between the royal houses of Valois and Plantagenet, but Edward was not interested. Very few possible crossing points remained before reaching Paris, and the English tried them all. Some way upriver from Meulan, French soldiers mocked the frustrated English by baring their backsides across the river. Philip VI resisted the temptation to cross the river, fearing that the English would suddenly attack Paris, and on the 13th he returned to his capital. Here the inhabitants could see smoke rising only a few kilometres to the west and south-west where English raiders were at work. Edward even issued a challenge to battle south of Paris and on 15 August Philip VI took his army to the southern wall, arraying them in readiness.

Edward's challenge was, of course, a ruse. The only way to join his Flemish allies was to rebuild one of the Seine bridges and Poissy was chosen. The town was devastated and its inhabitants, including King Philip's sister, had fled to Paris. English engineers now set to work and by the afternoon of the 15th a single beam had been laid across the gap. Philip VI heard the news and diverted a unit on its way from Amiens, but when they reached Poissy enough English troops were already across to drive them off. Still Edward III did not cross the Seine immediately and waited while his men spread devastation right up to the gates of Paris. But Philip VI would not be lured into premature action and similarly waited to see which way the English would turn.

'Soldiers at the Resurrection' on the Bohemian Vyssi Brod Altar. This panel was painted around 1350 and probably reflects Bohemian and other central European infantry quite accurately. (National Gallery, Prague)

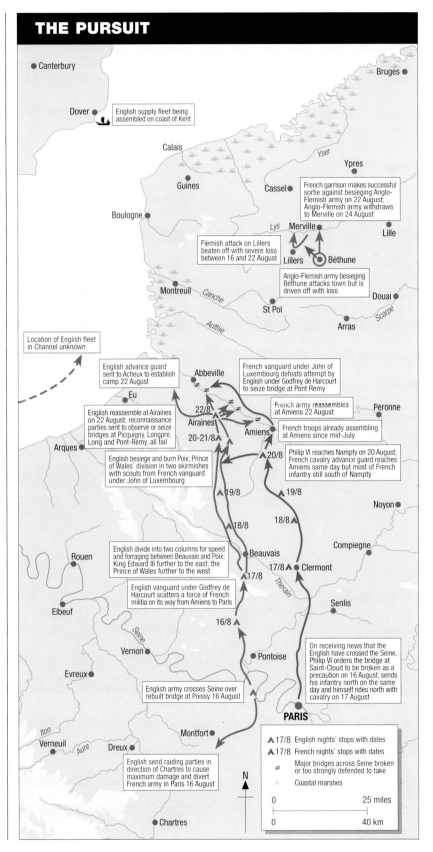

THE PURSUIT

- Canterbury
- Bruges
- Dover

English supply fleet being assembled on coast of Kent

- Calais
- Guines
- Cassel
- Ypres
- Yser
- Lys
- Merville
- Lille

French garrison makes successful sortie against besieging Anglo-Flemish army on 22 August; Anglo-Flemish army withdraws to Merville on 24 August

- Boulogne

Flemish attack on Lillers beaten off with severe loss between 16 and 22 August

- Lillers
- Béthune

Anglo-Flemish army besieging Béthune attacks town but is driven off with loss

- Montreuil
- Canche
- St Pol
- Douai
- Scarpe
- Authie
- Arras

Location of English fleet in Channel unknown

English advance guard sent to Acheux to establish camp 22 August

- Abbeville
- Eu

French vanguard under John of Luxembourg defeats attempt by English under Godfrey de Harcourt to seize bridge at Pont Remy

French army reassembles at Amiens 22 August

English reassemble at Airaines on 22 August; reconnaissance parties sent to observe or seize bridges at Picquigny, Longpré, Long and Pont-Remy, all fail

- 22/8
- Airaines
- Amiens
- Peronne

French troops already assembling at Amiens since mid-July

- Arques
- 20-21/8

English besiege and burn Poix; Prince of Wales' division in two skirmishes with scouts from French vanguard under John of Luxembourg

- 20/8

Philip VI reaches Nampty on 20 August; French cavalry advance guard reaches Amiens same day but most of French infantry still south of Nampty

- 19/8
- 19/8
- Noyon

- 18/8
- 18/8

- Compiegne

English divide into two columns for speed and foraging between Beauvais and Poix; King Edward III further to the east; the Prince of Wales further to the west

- Rouen
- Beauvais
- 17/8
- Clermont
- 17/8
- Therain

English vanguard under Godfrey de Harcourt scatters a force of French militia on its way from Amiens to Paris

- Senlis
- Elbeuf

- 16/8

- Seine
- Vernon
- Pontoise

On receiving news that the English have crossed the Seine, Philip VI orders the bridge at Saint-Cloud to be broken as a precaution on 16 August, sends his infantry north on the same day and himself rides north with cavalry on 17 August

- Evreux

English army crosses Seine over rebuilt bridge at Poissy 16 August

- Iton
- Verneuil
- Aure
- Dreux
- Montfort

PARIS

English send raiding parties in direction of Chartres to cause maximum damage and divert French army in Paris 16 August

▲ 17/8 English nights' stops with dates
▲ 17/8 French nights' stops with dates
≠ Major bridges across Seine broken or too strongly defended to take
  Coastal marshes

N

0 _____ 25 miles
0 _____ 40 km

- Chartres

TOP **A mid-14th-century northern Italian or French bascinet helmet with vervelles for its mail aventail and two hooked studs to secure the nose or face-covering bretache. (Private collection)**

ABOVE **A mid-14th-century German bascinet with a so-called 'dog-faced' visor. (National Museum, Budapest)**

The estuary of the River Somme between Saint-Valery-sur-Somme and the Blanchetaque ford. Since the area has been drained and a flood barrier erected between this spot and the sea, the flats are no longer tidal. In the 14th century they would have consisted of almost impassable mud, except where an outcrop of chalk provided a firmer footing. (Author's photograph)

The race to the Somme

On 16 August English marauders rode in the direction of Chartres to give the impression that Edward was heading southward, but instead Edward crossed the river and bolted north. As soon as this news was confirmed, Philip had the bridge at Saint-Cloud broken as a precaution and led his own army northward. He may have sent his infantry ahead before setting out with the cavalry on the 18th and on this first day Philip covered an impressive 55 kilometres.

In this race to the Somme the English had started first but the French won. Philip VI's army was reinforced by fresh contingents including those of Jaime I, King of Majorca. Each day the English averaged three times the ground they had covered in Normandy. Before reaching Beauvais the English vanguard under Godfrey de Harcourt scattered a force of Amiens militia on their way to Paris. The Prince of Wales now wanted to attack Beauvais itself, but Edward III told him to press on. North of Beauvais the people of Poix – probably the local militia – attacked English stragglers and this time part of Edward's army turned back to burn their town.

Soon the English had to abandon some of their baggage wagons for the sake of speed, but the countryside had been emptied of food stocks, forcing English foragers to scour far afield and slowing down Edward's march. The French now overtook the English, their leading troops reaching the Somme on 20 August. The infantry arrived later, but now the people of Picardy took heart and started attacking isolated groups of invaders. On the 20th Edward reached Camps-en-Amienois 25 kilometres south of the Somme. The English rearguard had, however, been delayed by attacking Poix and as a result the king had to wait for them to catch up. On the 22nd Edward halted his tired and hungry soldiers at the small fortified town of Airaines, whose garrison had been withdrawn to Pont-Remy. The main body of the French army reached Amiens that night. Philip VI now had numerical superiority and he

Pharaoh and his army as portrayed in the *Velislav Bible*, made around 1340. It is in a much more archaic style than the Vyssi Brod Altar. The arms, armour, costume and horse-harness are similarly old fashioned, perhaps reflecting styles that persisted in Bohemia before a major wave of German influence in the mid-14th century. (University Library, Ms. XXIII-C-24, f.70, Prague).

ordered the demolition or garrisoning of bridges over the Somme if they had fortifications.

Edward III had few options. On the 22nd he sent scouting parties to look at the Somme bridges, while a large force went to Acheux to establish a forward base. The largest scouting party, under Godfrey de Harcourt, tried to seize the bridge at Pont Remy but was thrown back. The Earl of Warwick also found that the bridges at Long, Longpré and Picquigny were too strongly defended. The English seemed to be trapped, but Edward was on home territory; Ponthieu had been his own county until confiscated by Philip VI at the outbreak of the war, and some of his commanders knew the area. Edward may have looked at the defences of Abbeville from Caubert Hill, while Warwick and de Harcourt attacked the town. They seem to have been driven off and the English certainly left Airaines in a hurry on the morning of the 23rd, the first French arriving only two hours after the last English departed for Acheux. At Oisemont local knights and militia made a stand, but were dispersed by English longbowmen.

Edward had a choice: he could fight where he was, retreat to Saint-Valéry and take ship home, or cross the Somme by the Blanchetaque ford. Its name referred to an outcrop of chalk which made the riverbed relatively firm and it would have been known to English commanders since it was maintained as an official crossing point at what was then the head of the Somme estuary. Various stories are told about information being bought from a French varlet captured at Oisemont, from a squire in the retinue of a Flemish knight in Edward's service, and from an Englishman who had lived near Oisemont for many years. So perhaps Edward III needed clarification about the ford's practicability for a large army with heavy wagons and, more importantly, about local tides.

Blanchetaque was certainly not an ideal spot for a large army to cross a major river. Nevertheless, before dawn on 24 August the English made a dash for the ford and reached Saigneville near its southern edge around dawn where they awaited low tide. Around eight in the morning it was possible for horsemen to cross, closely followed by infantry and wagons. The fact that they did so within an hour, suggests they crossed on a relatively wide front – a remarkable logistical feat.

The French had also set out at dawn, Philip VI sending Godemar du Fay to watch the north bank with 500 men-at-arms and 3,000 foot soldiers. He arrived as the leading English troops were crossing. Godemar du Fay's Genoese crossbowmen caused the English some losses, and his men-at-arms rode into the river to fight the enemy vanguard under Hugh Despenser, Reginald Cobham and the Earl of Northampton. But the French were too few, and some were pursued east towards Abbeville, others probably west to the high ground between Port-le-Grand and Noyelles. By the time the English rearguard came ashore the fighting was over. On the south bank the French vanguard

The oldest surviving structure in the little town of Crécy is the base of a cross erected by Eleanor of Aquitaine, mother of kings Richard and John of England, in 1159. This brick monument is now called the Lanterne des Morts and it stands at the foot of what was originally the road or track leading to Crécy Grange and Wadicourt. (Author's photograph)

CROSSING THE SOMME

The English crossed the Somme via the Blanchetaque ford. There were no bridges below Abbeville and this was the last ford before the estuary of the River Somme became too wide and too tidal to cross. Edward III's army seems to have crossed rapidly on a broad front, not only using the ford itself, where the baggage carts would have been concentrated, but either side as well. A small force of French men-at-arms and local French militia under Godemar du Fay, stiffened by a handful of professional Genoese crossbowmen, tried to resist the English but were overwhelmed after a brief, one-sided battle. Nevertheless, there was skirmishing even in the river, where the French men-at-arms came down to face the English vanguard.

under John of Luxembourg had captured a few English wagons but the tide was now rising fast; Edward III's army was north of the Somme and Philip was south.

There is still debate about the road Edward III took from Blanchetaque to Crécy. In the mid-14th century the coast north of the Somme was marshy and undrained, the little port of Le Crotoy being an island at high tide. The estuaries of the Somme, Maye and Authie were similarly undrained, their marshes reaching far inland, so there was no practical coastal road. The Forest of Crécy covered much of the area between the Somme and the Authie and was divided by the smaller River Maye, while further south the Forest of Cantâtre now only exists as isolated fragments. The rest of Ponthieu consisted of rolling agricultural land dotted with villages and windmills.

Edward III also had to consider the activities of his Flemish allies. On 16 August the French defenders in Béthune, commanded by Godfrey d'Annequin, beat off an assault in which Henry of Flanders was wounded. On the 22nd d'Annequin learned that a smaller Flemish force around Lillers had also suffered badly, so he risked a substantial and highly successful sortie. The Flemish militias started quarrelling among themselves and on the 24th, the day the English crossed the Somme, they abandoned their siege and retreated to Merville.

That same day an English force under Sir Hugh Despenser took Noyelles, Le Crotoy and Rue, but there no sign of an English fleet bringing urgently needed supplies. Philip had refused to be lured into attempting a crossing at Blanchetaque and the English army was not only tired, but even its shoes were wearing out. On the 25th Edward learned of his allies' retreat and Philip returned to Abbeville to decide his next move. It was probably at this point that Edward III decided that since his army could no longer outrun the French, it would make a stand at nearby Crécy. So Warwick, Cobham, Suffolk and Godfrey de Harcourt were sent ahead as the main English force moved slowly along the only road through the forest towards a low hill overlooking the village of Crécy, keeping as far as possible from the French in Abbeville.

THE BATTLEFIELD

Edward had selected a position north of the shallow valley of the Maye. It was on the edge of an undulating plain, with Estrées to the east and Wadicourt to the north-east, both villages probably being surrounded by orchards. The low ridge between Wadicourt and Crécy was about two kilometres long with a windmill overlooking Crécy itself. Behind the ridge was Crécy-Grange Wood, partially covering the English rear and right flank. The Vallée des Clercs was little more than a dip in the prevailing high ground, leading from Wadicourt to the Maye. It was about two kilometres long and no more than 35 metres lower than the surrounding plateau at its lowest point. Some French scholars believe that there were three ancient or medieval cultivation terraces or raidillons in front of the English centre, though these are not mentioned in original sources. There is a bump towards the bottom of the slope but this would not have been an obstacle to a cavalry charge and still less to infantry. If a substantial hedge existed, it is likely to have been on top of the ridge.

Among the various infantrymen carved by Giovanni de Campione c. 1360 in the southern portal of Santa Maria Maggiore is this man. He has what appears to be a heavy mace, a basilard dagger and a large tabulaccio shield. Foot soldiers equipped in this manner would almost certainly have served alongside the Genoese crossbowmen at Crécy. (Santa Maria Maggiore, Bergamo; author's photograph)

RIGHT The probable site of the English fortified encampment or ring of wagons on the plateau north-east of Crécy. The modern buildings of Crécy Grange farm can be seen on the right, beneath the edge of Crécy Grange Wood. The battlefield is just beyond the skyline on the left. (Author's photograph)

King Edward drew up his battle array at an almost leisurely pace during the morning of 26 August. The men were grouped into the same three divisions in which they had marched. The vanguard under the nominal authority of the young Prince of Wales, though supervised by Godfrey de Harcourt, was placed closest to Crécy and the anticipated French approach, the central battle or division under the king moving past them to take up position on the ridge between Crécy and Wadicourt. The rearguard, under the command of the earls of Northampton and Arundel, moved further still to place itself between the king and Wadicourt. When seen from Crécy village it still formed a vanguard, a centre and a rearguard, but all commentators assume that Edward knew that the French would attack from the Vallée des Clercs. The horses were put inside a field fortification of wagons behind the centre-right flank and in front of the army, certainly on its right flank, and a series of scattered pot-holes about a foot square were dug to disrupt an enemy cavalry charge. The Prince of Wales' division on the right wing seems to have been some way down the slope.

The precise position of the English archers is another subject of debate. They were probably placed on each side of the army like wings and close to the men-at-arms. They may also have fallen back as the French attacked since it was not their task to engage the enemy hand-to-hand. Many may, as the contemporary Italian chronicler Villani stated, have ended up behind the men-at-arms. Froissart's use of the term herce or 'harrow' is still not fully understood, but what historians have apparently failed to notice is a similarity between Froissart's herce and a formation called El Haz, 'the closely packed bundle', in a 14th-century Spanish military treatise by Don Juan Manuel. Many of Froissart's informants would, of course, subsequently campaign in Spain with the Black Prince. Overall the evidence suggests that the archers were in relatively close-packed units which could move around in a controlled manner.

Then there is the question of the English guns, apparently on the English right wing. They are likely to have been small bombards, which were already used in parts of southern Europe to defend field fortifications. Edward III's baggage train was close to Crécy Grange and the wood, probably surrounded by wagons with a single opening but close enough for the archers to be rapidly resupplied with arrows during the battle.

TOP **So-called 'Hauberk of St Wenceslas', 13th-14th century (Cathedral Treasury, Prague)**

ABOVE **Tooled hardened leather rerebrace upper-arm defence found in London, mid-14th century. (London Museum, London)**

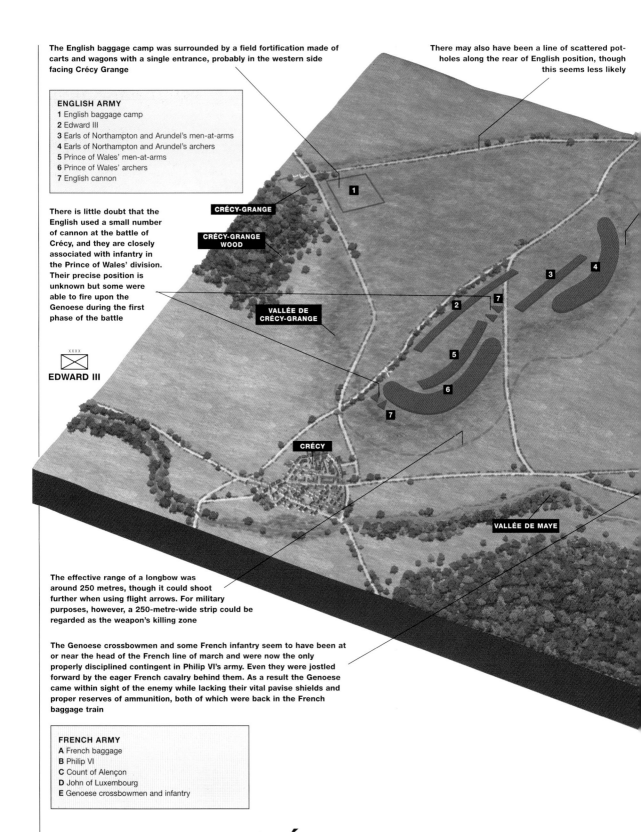

The English baggage camp was surrounded by a field fortification made of carts and wagons with a single entrance, probably in the western side facing Crécy Grange

There may also have been a line of scattered potholes along the rear of English position, though this seems less likely

ENGLISH ARMY
1 English baggage camp
2 Edward III
3 Earls of Northampton and Arundel's men-at-arms
4 Earls of Northampton and Arundel's archers
5 Prince of Wales' men-at-arms
6 Prince of Wales' archers
7 English cannon

There is little doubt that the English used a small number of cannon at the battle of Crécy, and they are closely associated with infantry in the Prince of Wales' division. Their precise position is unknown but some were able to fire upon the Genoese during the first phase of the battle

CRÉCY-GRANGE

CRÉCY-GRANGE WOOD

VALLÉE DE CRÉCY-GRANGE

EDWARD III

CRÉCY

VALLÉE DE MAYE

The effective range of a longbow was around 250 metres, though it could shoot further when using flight arrows. For military purposes, however, a 250-metre-wide strip could be regarded as the weapon's killing zone

The Genoese crossbowmen and some French infantry seem to have been at or near the head of the French line of march and were now the only properly disciplined contingent in Philip VI's army. Even they were jostled forward by the eager French cavalry behind them. As a result the Genoese came within sight of the enemy while lacking their vital pavise shields and proper reserves of ammunition, both of which were back in the French baggage train

FRENCH ARMY
A French baggage
B Philip VI
C Count of Alençon
D John of Luxembourg
E Genoese crossbowmen and infantry

THE BATTLE OF CRÉCY 26 AUGUST 1346:
initial positions

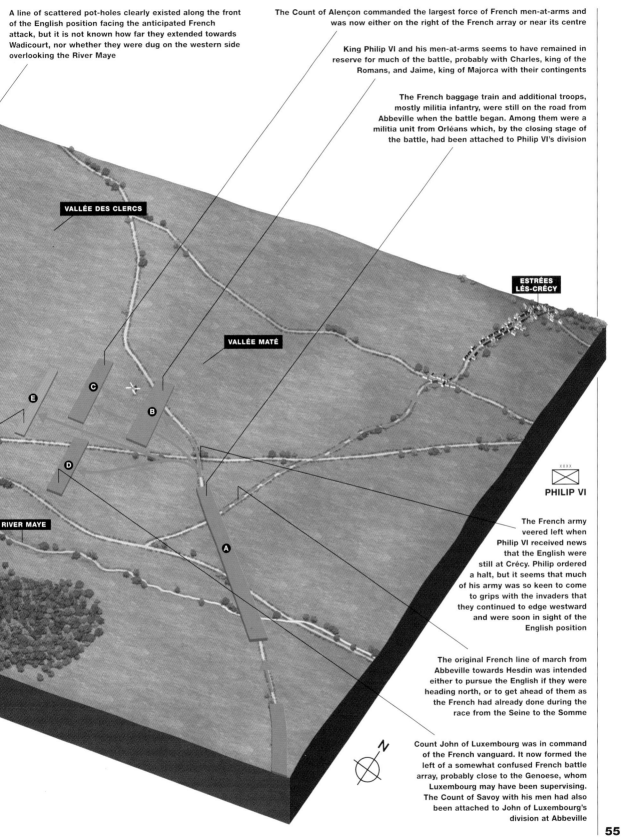

A line of scattered pot-holes clearly existed along the front of the English position facing the anticipated French attack, but it is not known how far they extended towards Wadicourt, nor whether they were dug on the western side overlooking the River Maye

The Count of Alençon commanded the largest force of French men-at-arms and was now either on the right of the French array or near its centre

King Philip VI and his men-at-arms seems to have remained in reserve for much of the battle, probably with Charles, king of the Romans, and Jaime, king of Majorca with their contingents

The French baggage train and additional troops, mostly militia infantry, were still on the road from Abbeville when the battle began. Among them were a militia unit from Orléans which, by the closing stage of the battle, had been attached to Philip VI's division

VALLÉE DES CLERCS

VALLÉE MATÉ

ESTRÉES LÉS-CRÉCY

E

C

B

D

A

RIVER MAYE

PHILIP VI

The French army veered left when Philip VI received news that the English were still at Crécy. Philip ordered a halt, but it seems that much of his army was so keen to come to grips with the invaders that they continued to edge westward and were soon in sight of the English position

The original French line of march from Abbeville towards Hesdin was intended either to pursue the English if they were heading north, or to get ahead of them as the French had already done during the race from the Seine to the Somme

Count John of Luxembourg was in command of the French vanguard. It now formed the left of a somewhat confused French battle array, probably close to the Genoese, whom Luxembourg may have been supervising. The Count of Savoy with his men had also been attached to John of Luxembourg's division at Abbeville

55

Crécy Grange Wood on the left and the probable location of the English camp beyond the clump of trees in the centre, as seen from the top of a wooden tower recently built almost on the spot of the medieval windmill. The road in the foreground would have marked the rear of the English line, which would have been facing in the opposite direction to this photograph. (Author's photograph)

On the day of battle King Edward rose early and, with the Prince of Wales, heard mass and took communion. The army would have done the same before taking up their positions. Food was cooked within the baggage train, the fighting men being allowed to leave their positions a few at a time to eat and relieve themselves. Each archer marked his position with his bow, each man-at-arms with his helmet. Edward's final order, once the French came in sight, was that no prisoners would be taken, nor was any man to leave his position to look for loot.

The French march to Crécy was not the disorganised scramble that some historians have maintained. Nor were King Philip VI's plans as incompetent as some believe. Nevertheless, he did not enjoy the same control over his troops as Edward III. Having returned to Abbeville from Blanchetaque on the 24th, Philip VI remained throughout the 25th, probably because several contingents were still on their way to join him. Jaime I, the exiled king of Majorca, had already arrived, as had John of Luxembourg's son Charles, who had been proclaimed king of the Romans in July 1346, as well as Edward III's brother-in-law Count John of Hainault and several minor German princelings; the Count of Savoy and his brother Louis arriving on the 25th. Philip also knew the siege of Béthune had been abandoned and that the English could not immediately join their Flemish allies.

The French line of march is another of Crécy's unanswered questions. Certainly Philip's force was now so large that it was divided between Abbeville and Saint-Riquier. He knew that the pursuit must continue next day and his army set out at dawn, leaving their cannon behind as they had to move fast. Smoke was rising from the direction of Noyelles and the vanguard of the French headed in that direction, but scouts would soon have reported that the English were no longer there. At this point the French army, strung along the road from Abbeville to Noyelles, were ordered to turn right towards Crécy and Hesdin. The vanguard and perhaps Philip VI seem to have been more than halfway to Noyelles before they turned along what came to be called the 'Valois Path' before reaching the English route, traditionally known as 'Le Chemin de l'Armée'. King Philip now placed his infantry ahead of the cavalry as a precaution against ambush as they marched between the forests of Crécy and Cantâtre, presumably separating the Genoese crossbowmen from their pavise shields in the baggage train. Around this point a reconnaissance party was also sent ahead under Miles de Noyers, the royal standard-bearer, Jean de Beaumont and Henri le Moine of Basle.

Much of the French army was strung along the road from Abbeville and some took various lanes east of the Forest of Cantâtre, while others may even have headed direct from Abbeville towards Hesdin. This would account for the confused state of the army when it was east of Crécy. The mounted men-at-arms now formed a disorderly mass behind the more disciplined Genoese infantry, their commanders still believing that they were trying to catch the English as the latter retreated north. The medieval road itself probably followed the line of a Roman road near Cancy, Mancheville, Fontaine-sur-Maye and Estrées-les-Crécy.

The head of the French army was probably passing Fontaine when, in mid-afternoon, the reconnaissance party told Philip that his enemy held a strongly defended position to the left of his line of march, perhaps within

Another marginal illustration from the *Luttrell Psalter* of *c.*1340 shows an archer with a full-length longbow, what appears to be a blunted target arrow and a ballock dagger at his waist. (*Luttrell Psalter*, British Library, Ms. Add. 42130, f. 45r, London)

This French manuscript illustration of an attack on a castle or fortified town was made over a generation after the battle of Crécy. It does, however, show a small cannon in a heavy wooden cradle in the lower left corner. The English guns at Crécy would probably have been of this type. (British Library, Ms. Cotton Nero E.II, London)

THE ENGLISH MAKE PREPARATIONS NEAR CRÉCY

The English army had time to make a strongly fortified position on the ridge between Crécy and Wadicourt. The ordinary soldiers are reported to have dug a series of small scattered pot-holes in front of their positions. These were intended to trip the enemy's horses and the idea is said to have been learned from the Scots. Relatively small holes would have been easier to make, less visible and thus harder to avoid, than long ditches. By making even a few horses fall they would also effectively disrupt the cohesion and momentum of an enemy charge. At the southern end of the gentle slope overlooking what became known as the Vallée des Clercs was a windmill. Behind it there may have been a dense hedge running alongside the track from Crécy to Wadicourt. King Edward himself is said to have ridden around the English positions, encouraging his men but not himself wearing any armour.

This panel from a particularly finely carved Easter Sepulchre altar front, made around 1345, shows a fully armoured man-at-arms from the Rhineland. Many of the allied cavalry in Philip VI's army would have used such armour. (Musée de l'Oeuvre Notre Dame, Strasbourg; author's photograph)

sight of the front of the French army. There seems to have been some delay before Philip ordered a halt. Perhaps he had planned to make camp at Estrées. The Genoese infantry under Carlo Grimaldi and Odone Doria were tired after a long march. Behind them great numbers of men-at-arms were now somewhat disorganised. The bulk of the French militia infantry and the baggage were further back, while hordes of local people filled the lanes between the Somme and Crécy in hope of striking a blow. Other contingents may only just have reached Abbeville.

While his marshals rode up and down, trying to stop the men-at-arms jostling forward in their eagerness to punish an enemy which had wrought such devastation, Philip VI held council with his senior commanders. He received conflicting advice, the reconnaissance party urging him to wait until tomorrow before attacking the well-prepared English position; some suggesting that they press on to Labroye castle, where they could reorganise and block the English march northwards; others demanded an immediate attack to avoid a repeat of previous stand-offs. Philip took the latter course, perhaps realising that it would be almost impossible to make his enthusiastic army abandon the field within sight of their foe.

Once Philip decided to attack, the disarray seemed to get worse as units crossed each other's paths, pushing those ahead still further forward. As the chronicler Froissart said, 'This disorder was entirely caused by pride, every man wishing to surpass his neighbour, in spite of the marshals' words.' Few of their commanders had experience of full-scale battle but the men were confident. French knighthood had the highest reputation in Christendom and there were many hardened veterans in their ranks, particularly among the Genoese.

The French force numbered roughly the same as the English troops facing them on the other side of the Vallée des Clercs, but in terms of men actually in the line of battle they may have been outnumbered. Philip certainly knew about the English longbowmen but perhaps believed that his Genoese crossbowmen could counter-balance them with sustained and accurate fire. The English archers were, after all, virtually unarmoured. Philip may similarly have expected a short battle, so starting late in the afternoon would not be a problem.

The French array is perhaps Crécy's biggest mystery, with sources mentioning from four to nine units or lines of men. Apart from the well-organised Genoese, Philip's army may actually have consisted simply of two, three or four unwieldy cavalry divisions, perhaps with infantry on their flanks or still arriving from the rear. Men-at-arms under the Duke of Alençon and John of Luxembourg formed the first line, probably with Alençon on the right and John of Luxembourg in support of the Genoese. Philip VI's own contingent, plus those of the king of Majorca and other senior noblemen including John of Luxembourg's son Charles, may have formed a reserve.

THE BATTLE

The battlefield of Crécy looking from where the windmill stood, over the Prince of Wales' position in the foreground, towards a modern beet factory where the Vallée des Clercs meets the small River Maye. The village of Fontaine-sur-Maye is in the centre of the skyline. The initial attack by Genoese cross-bowmen was up this hill, followed by the first cavalry charge of the Duke of Alençon's division. (Author's photograph)

The Prince of Wales' division was probably closest to the French. The sacred French Oriflamme was now unfurled, indicating that no invader should be taken prisoner, and around 5pm Philip VI ordered the Genoese forward without their pavises – in direct contravention of their normal tactics in Italy. Though it was common for infantry to form the front line in Italian warfare, the Genoese were used to serving in highly structured armies in which they were closely supported by equally professional cavalry. Not surprisingly they were not keen on advancing at the end of a long march, without proper preparation, without their pavises or adequate reserves of ammunition and with the lowering sun in their eyes. Their officers' complaints to the Count of Alençon were

Hesdin

Canche

Authie

Labroye

Rue

Maye

(S) Wadicourt

(P)

Le Crotoy

Crécy · (X) Estrées

Forest of Crécy

Fontaines-sur-Maye

St Valéry

Marcheville

Nouvion · Forest l'Abbaye

Labroye

(Q)

(R)

Noyelles

Canchy

(U)

(V)

(L)

(W)

Blanchetaque Ford

(T)

(W)

Saigneville

(W) St Riquier

(J)

(O)

(K)

(M)

(O) Abbeville

(I)

Caubert Hill

Acheux

(E)

Pont-Remy

(N)

(D)

Long (B)

(G)

Longpré

Somme

(F)

(A)

(C)

(H)

(G)

Oisemont

Airaines

Picquigny

N

0 — 5 miles

0 — 5 km

Legend

⌣ Bridges over Somme either broken or too strongly defended to take

● Towns, villages & hamlets

Tidal flats & riverine marshes

🌳 Woods & forest

A Edward III and bulk of the English army at Airaines 22 August

B French vanguard marches from Amiens to defend bridges and north bank of the Somme; defeats English at Pont Remy and continues to Abbeville 22 August

C English reconnaissance force under Earl of Warwick finds bridges at Picquigny, Longpré and Long either broken or too strongly defended to take 22 August

D Attempt by English force under Godfrey de Harcourt to seize bridge at Pont Remy defeated by French vanguard under John of Luxembourg 22 August

E English under Edward III, Earl of Warwick and Godfrey de Harcourt approach Abbeville; detachment led by Warwick and De Harcourt attack bridge but are defeated by garrison, local militia and probably John of Luxembourg; Edward III observes Abbeville from Caubert Hill; English return to Airaines 22 August

F English diversionary raids to confuse French, then march hurriedly to Oisemont and Acheux early morning 23 August

G Main French army from Amiens and vanguard under John of Luxembourg from Abbeville, perhaps with Abbeville militia and garrison, reaches Airaines two hours after English have left 23 August

H Local French feudal and militia forces confront English outside Oisemont but are defeated; village is plundered and Edward III spends night of 23 August at Oisemont

I English make predawn march to Blanchetaque ford on 24 August, avoiding valleys and wooded areas but have to await low tide around 8 o'clock

J French force under Godemar du Fay sent to guard Blanchetaque ford arrive as first English are crossing

K English cross the Somme on a wide front centred upon the Blanchetaque ford during morning of 24 August

L English fight way ashore and scatter French defenders; some of latter probably retreat to Abbeville, others to Noyelles

M French vanguard under John of Luxembourg reaches Blanchetaque and clashes with last English troops to cross ford

N Philip VI leads main French army toward Blanchetaque ford but returns to Abbeville because rising tide makes immediate pursuit of English impractical

O Philip VI and main French army spend 25 August in Abbeville and Saint-Riquier while additional reinforcements arrive

P English foraging force under Sir Hugh Despenser takes and sacks Noyelles, Rue and Le Crotoy, the latter two at low tide; no sign of the expected English ships at Le Crotoy

Q English adopt defensive position and use remainder of 24 August resting; Edward III spends night at Labroye

R English army marches between Forests of Crécy and Cantâtre to Crécy 25 August

S English adopt strong defensive position between Crécy and Wadicourt

T French army leaves Abbeville at dawn on 26 August towards Noyelles etc. which is still burning

U French vanguard and perhaps main division under Philip VI turn right along so-called 'Valois path' when King realised that the English have left the area

V Philip VI puts the available troops of the French army in marching battle array near Le Titre, with Genoese infantry in the vanguard; also sends a reconnaissance unit led by four knights to find the English

W Rear sections of the French army probably turn right before reaching the Forest of Cantâtre, to rejoin the rest of the army south of the Forest of Crécy, causing considerable confusion

X French army now very crowded and disorganized, except for the Genoese infantry in the front, reach between Fontaines-sur-Maye and Estrées-lès-Crécy where Philip learns from his reconnaissance unit that the English are in a prepared position between Crécy and Wadicourt; Philip VI calls a halt while some of the French army are within sight of the enemy, and discusses the situation with his senior commanders

The Vallée des Clercs from the site of Edward III's windmill, with the villages of Estrées-les-Crécy behind the trees in the distance. The three clumps of trees in the middle distance on the right may mark the site of another windmill, perhaps at the centre of the French position. (Author's photograph)

ignored, but were subsequently taken as evidence of the Genoese' supposed treachery. Nevertheless, they formed up under the command of Ottone Doria with the Prince of Wales' division as their target. The 2,000 to 6,000 Genoese were also greatly outnumbered by the opposing longbowmen; perhaps even by those of the Prince of Wales' division alone.

To the sound of trumpets and drums, the Genoese crossbowmen and spearmen moved forward in three stages, each pause being signalled by a shout that enabled the foot soldiers to adjust their ranks. Legend recalled two great crows which flew over the battlefield as they advanced, but more significant was a sudden rain storm – the first in six weeks. This made the ground slippery, and to this day the bottom of the Vallée des Clercs remains very muddy days after rain for some 250 metres from its junction with the River Maye. The rain also soaked the strings of the Genoese crossbows, making them lose considerable power. Jean de Venette stated that the English longbowmen took the strings from their bows and kept them dry beneath their helmets. However, this simply could not be done with a crossbow, and only the stretching of the Genoese crossbow strings can account for the ease with which the English longbowmen outranged their opponents. It also enabled the English to take advantage of their weapons' only real superiority; the rapidity with which they could shoot and their ability to rain heavy arrows from a high trajectory. In terms of accuracy, range and penetrating power the advantage should otherwise have been with the Genoese.

The Genoese role should have been to disrupt the enemy line with crossbow bolts, whereupon the supporting cavalry would take advantage

ABOVE **The road from Crécy towards Wadicourt, which lies behind the trees in the distance. This part of the English position was held by the earls of Northampton and Arundel on the left wing. (Author's photograph)**

LEFT **Detail of a German effigy of a knight in somewhat old-fashioned costume over a coat-of-plates, with a substantial dagger on his right hip. It dates from around 1358. Comparable armour was clearly worn in many parts of France. (Kirchzarten Church; author's photograph)**

of any breaks. In fact the Genoese shot the third time they halted, about 150 metres from the English. They did so uphill with a low sun almost directly in their eyes, a major disadvantage for men who aimed directly at their targets rather than dropping arrows on them. As they shot, the Genoese were hit by an arrow storm from the Prince of Wales' division to which the English guns added noise, terror and casualties. Froissart stated that they made 'two or three discharges on the Genoese', each gun firing once as it was not possible to reload such primitive weapons any faster. Villani agreed that their impact was considerable, and maintained that the bombards continued to fire upon French cavalry later in the battle: 'The English guns cast iron balls by means of fire ... They made a noise like thunder and caused much loss in men and horses ... The Genoese were continually hit by the archers and the gunners ... [by end of battle] the whole plain was covered by men struck down by arrows and cannon balls.'

Without their pavises, outshot and outranged by their opponents, the Genoese wavered, then streamed back. They are said to have been attacked by the French men-at-arms who were supervising them and although this seems unlikely, the Count of Alençon apparently concluded that the Italians had been bribed to betray King Philip. On the other hand, Jean de Venette maintained that some men-at-arms attacked their own infantry, 'though all the while the crossbowmen were excusing themselves with great cries'. The English ability to shoot further volleys into this confusion also suggests that the cavalry in question were with the Genoese during their initial advance.

The idea that Philip VI ordered his men-at-arms to ride down the broken Genoese is almost inconceivable since it would have ruined the cohesion of a cavalry charge. More likely the Count of Alençon advanced when he saw

BELOW, RIGHT **These little carved figures on a 14th-century English misericorde represent monsters or demons with birds' leg's. The upper parts of their bodies, however, are men wearing typical costume of the period, carrying small round buckler shields and in one case a heavy basilard dagger. (St Mary's Church, Lancaster; author's photograph)**

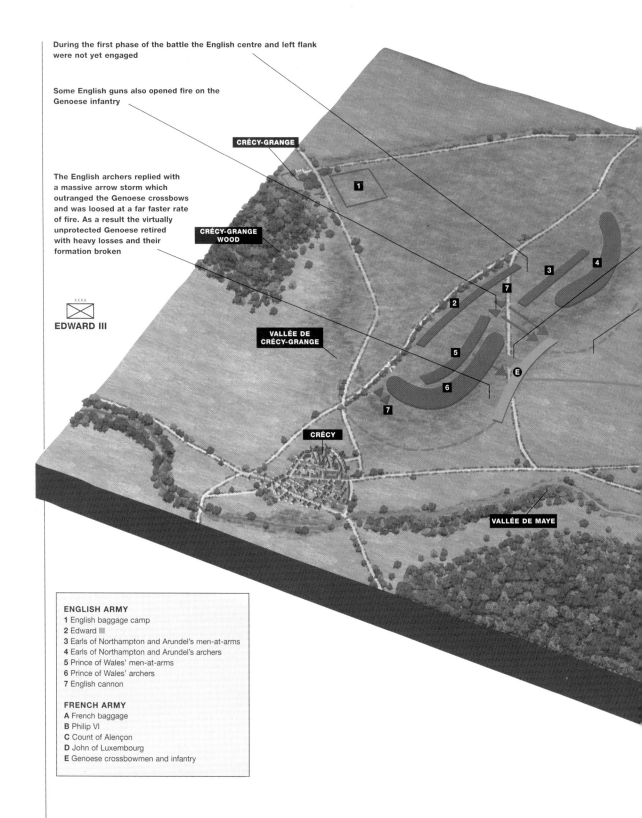

During the first phase of the battle the English centre and left flank were not yet engaged

Some English guns also opened fire on the Genoese infantry

CRÉCY-GRANGE

1

The English archers replied with a massive arrow storm which outranged the Genoese crossbows and was loosed at a far faster rate of fire. As a result the virtually unprotected Genoese retired with heavy losses and their formation broken

CRÉCY-GRANGE WOOD

3

4

7

2

xxxx
EDWARD III

VALLÉE DE CRÉCY-GRANGE

5

E

6

7

CRÉCY

VALLÉE DE MAYE

ENGLISH ARMY
1 English baggage camp
2 Edward III
3 Earls of Northampton and Arundel's men-at-arms
4 Earls of Northampton and Arundel's archers
5 Prince of Wales' men-at-arms
6 Prince of Wales' archers
7 English cannon

FRENCH ARMY
A French baggage
B Philip VI
C Count of Alençon
D John of Luxembourg
E Genoese crossbowmen and infantry

THE BATTLE OF CRÉCY 26 AUGUST 1346:
defeat of the Genoese and Alençon

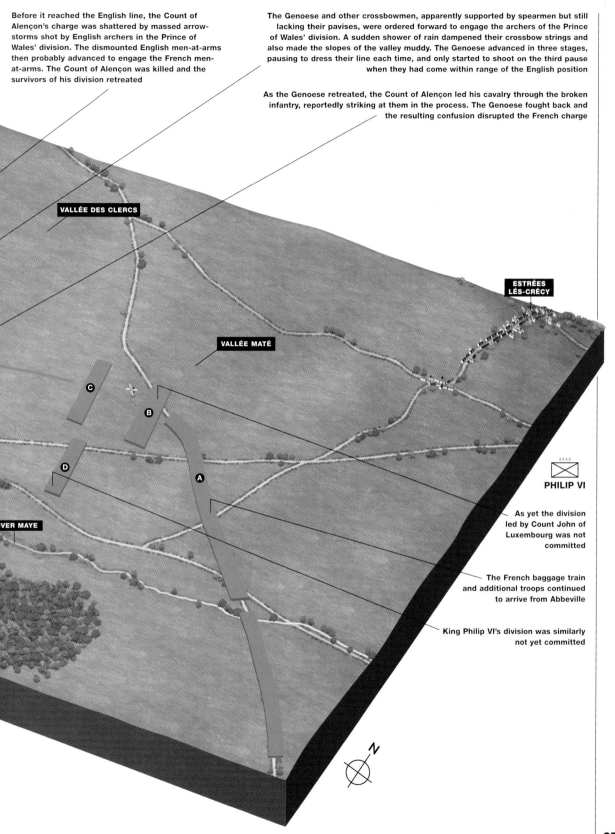

Before it reached the English line, the Count of Alençon's charge was shattered by massed arrow-storms shot by English archers in the Prince of Wales' division. The dismounted English men-at-arms then probably advanced to engage the French men-at-arms. The Count of Alençon was killed and the survivors of his division retreated

The Genoese and other crossbowmen, apparently supported by spearmen but still lacking their pavises, were ordered forward to engage the archers of the Prince of Wales' division. A sudden shower of rain dampened their crossbow strings and also made the slopes of the valley muddy. The Genoese advanced in three stages, pausing to dress their line each time, and only started to shoot on the third pause when they had come within range of the English position

As the Genoese retreated, the Count of Alençon led his cavalry through the broken infantry, reportedly striking at them in the process. The Genoese fought back and the resulting confusion disrupted the French charge

VALLÉE DES CLERCS

ESTRÉES LÉS-CRÉCY

VALLÉE MATÉ

C

B

D

A

VER MAYE

PHILIP VI

As yet the division led by Count John of Luxembourg was not committed

The French baggage train and additional troops continued to arrive from Abbeville

King Philip VI's division was similarly not yet committed

N

an opportunity to hit the English, perhaps in the belief that they would be unready after having just confronted the Genoese. Equally clearly his men-at-arms took no care to avoid the scattered infantry and caused additional casualties as they rode through. Whether or not the French and Genoese really came to blows remains unknown. Carlo Grimaldi himself was severely wounded, though it is not clear when he was hit.

Philip VI now only had cavalry readily available. They, however, had to charge uphill across muddy fields, through the broken remnants of their own infantry against an enemy flushed with victory and protected with virtually invisible pot-holes to trip the French horses. Not surprisingly the Count of Alençon's first attack failed. He seems to have ridden past the English archers, aiming for the Prince of Wales' banner, which was surrounded by dismounted men-at-arms. But before he reached the target his cavalry was hit by one or more arrow storms. Numerous horses were struck, while others tripped in potholes, the dead and wounded animals lined up like piglets suckling a sow.

The arrows caused far more damage to horses than to their riders, but many of the latter were thrown as the charge collapsed. Formation was lost, horses reared, fled or panicked and lay down, refusing to move. As Jean le Bel described it, 'The arrows of the English were directed with such marvellous skill at the horsemen that their mounts refused to advance a step. Some leapt backwards stung to madness, some reared hideously, some turned their rear quarters towards the enemy, others merely let themselves fall to the ground, and their riders could do nothing about it.' The English men-at-arms then advanced and attacked the confused Frenchmen. Some sources maintain that the French reached the English position and that the Count of Alençon touched the Prince of Wales' banner before being cut down, but this is almost certainly a heroic myth.

John of Luxembourg's men-at-arms were the next into the fray, perhaps moving forward as their commander realised that Alençon was in trouble. Certainly he was aware of the situation and asked the whereabouts of his son Charles, king of the Romans. Some of John's advisers reportedly urged him to flee, but instead the near-blind old warrior ordered his companions to tie their horses' bridles to his before leading him against the Prince of Wales. According to Froissart his last request had been, 'Je vous requers tres especialement que vous me

Only one statue representing the early 14th-century militia of Ghent now survives. It was made around 1340 and originally stood on the city's belfry. The militiaman's arms and armour are just as up to date as those of a knight, as would be expected in a rich Flemish city like Ghent. (Stonework Museum, St Bavon's Abbey, Ghent)

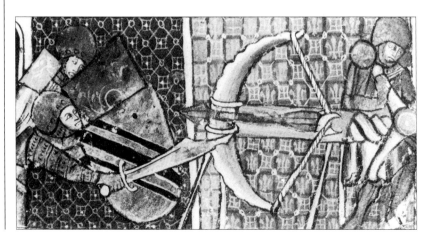

The *Liber de Nobilitatibus, Sapientiis et Prudentiis Regum* by Walter de Milemete, made in 1326, is best known for its very early representation of a cannon, but it also contains pictures of other siege machines. This giant frame-mounted crossbow is, like the cannon, exaggerated and inaccurate, but includes the screw system to span such a weapon. (Christ Church Library, Ms. 92, f. 69, Oxford)

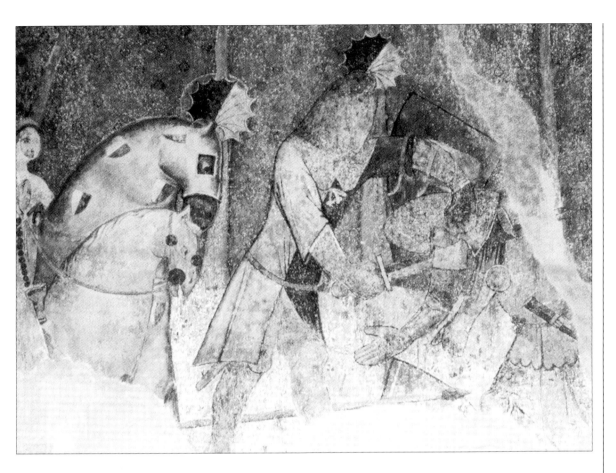

Tristan slays an enemy knight in a series of French wall-paintings illustrating the *Roman de Tristan et Iseult* made in the mid-or late-14th century. Tristan's armour is old-fashioned, whereas that of his enemy includes a number of modern features, as well as the man's shorter surcoat. (St Floret Castle; author's photograph)

meniez si'avant que me puisse ferir un coup d'epee' (I specially request you to place me so far forward that I am able to strike a sword-blow).

Whatever the truth, John of Luxembourg's men-at-arms now attacked with their war cry of 'Prague!' and did so with greater success. According to Froissart: 'Certain lords and knights and esquires on the French side, in addition to certain Germans and Savoyards, did break through the archers in the Prince of Wales' division and came up against his men-at-arms whom they attacked with swords, man-to-man, with great valour ... for all the flower of English chivalry was there around the Prince.' In the resulting mêlée John of Luxembourg and his companions were dragged from their horses and killed.

That morning King Philip had given a black charger to John of Hainault, who in turn gave it to his standard-bearer, Sir John de Fusselles. On this great horse Fusselles barged right through the English line and came out the other side. But the animal was struck by an arrow and fell into a ditch, trapping its rider until Fusselles' page rode around the English position and freed his master before they returned 'by a different way.'

During John of Luxembourg's charge Prince Edward was forced to his knees before being rescued by his standard bearer, Sir Richard FitzSimon. The latter is said to have put down the banner to defend his prince, but this would have been contrary to a standard bearer's duties and may have been a legend to explain why the banner briefly fell. Flemish sources maintain that the Count of Hainault pulled the banner from FitzSimon's

THE DEFEAT OF THE GENOESE

Genoese and French crossbowmen, supported by other infantry but not protected by their large pavise shields, which were still in the baggage train, were sent against the Prince of Wales' position at the south-western end or right flank of the English position. This was the first French attack and was intended to break up the English line with crossbow bolts. A heavy shower of rain had slackened the crossbows' string, which, unlike the strings of English longbows, could not be removed and replaced in battle. As a result, the range of the Genoese weapons was significantly reduced and this, coupled with a lack of pavise shields behind which they normally reloaded their weapons, made the crossbowmen highly vulnerable. Within a few minutes they were suffering severe casualties from the English arrow storms and were forced to pull back, only to be ridden down by French cavalry who thought that the retreating Genoese had turned traitor.

hands until he and Sir Thomas Daniel raised it again. Meanwhile, the Earl of Northampton received a message from Godfrey de Harcourt and sent his nearest unit, commanded by the Earl of Arundel, to help the prince. The messenger may have been the same Sir Thomas Norwich who also asked help from the king who, according to Froissart, asked, 'Sir Thomas, is my son dead, fallen or so wounded that he cannot help himself?' This was not the case, so Edward III famously replied; 'I order that the lad be allowed to earn his spurs, for it is my wish if the day be his, the glory of it belong to him and those in whose charge I have entrusted him.' Most likely Edward, from his position on top of the ridge, saw Arundel's counter-attack and realised that the danger was over.

Alençon and Luxembourg were both now dead, but the French made as many as 13 further cavalry charges, each leaving their dead and wounded in front of the English position. Most were against the Prince of Wales' division, though the Earl of Northampton was also attacked. In the centre Edward III merely seems to have sent reinforcements where needed, including the Bishop of Durham and 20 knights to help his son.

The French attacks became spasmodic and disjoined until, as dusk fell, Edward III ordered the English to advance. The horses were brought and, after forming into conrois formations, the English men-at-arms charged. Most of what remained of the French army fled, although Philip VI's own followers stood firm, with 50 to 70 lances or cavalry units and the Orléans militia. Philip twice had horses killed beneath him and he may have been struck in the jaw by an arrow. His standard-bearer was killed, the royal banner and the Oriflamme both being captured. Fighting continued until dark as the English, Welsh and Cornish infantry moved forward to kill the wounded and stunned that lay around the Vallée des Clercs. Belated efforts were made to capture some of the enemy alive, Godfrey de Harcourt unsuccessfully trying to save the life of his brother John de Harcourt.

This effigy is thought to be the earliest carved from alabaster in England. It dates from around 1340 and is also interesting because the knight seems to wear a coat-of-plates, indicated by horizontal hoops, either beneath or attached to the interior of his surcoat. Otherwise his equipment is old-fashioned. (Hanbury Church; author's photograph)

The knights jousting on this carved wooden misericorde, spurred on by a drummer and a trumpeter, are equipped with the latest armour. It was carved in the mid- to late-14th century and illustrates the huge changes that took place around the time of Crécy. (Great Malvern Priory; author's photograph)

Eventually the Count of Hainault, having survived John of Luxembourg's charge and perhaps others as well, grabbed Philip VI's bridle and dragged him off the field. With a handful of followers they fled to Labroye castle, where the king had some difficulty convincing the garrison of his identity. Next day Philip went to Doullens. Back on the battlefield King Edward refused to allow his men to pursue. He probably knew that several French contingents had not yet reached the scene of carnage. Edward III reportedly had the famous windmill set alight to

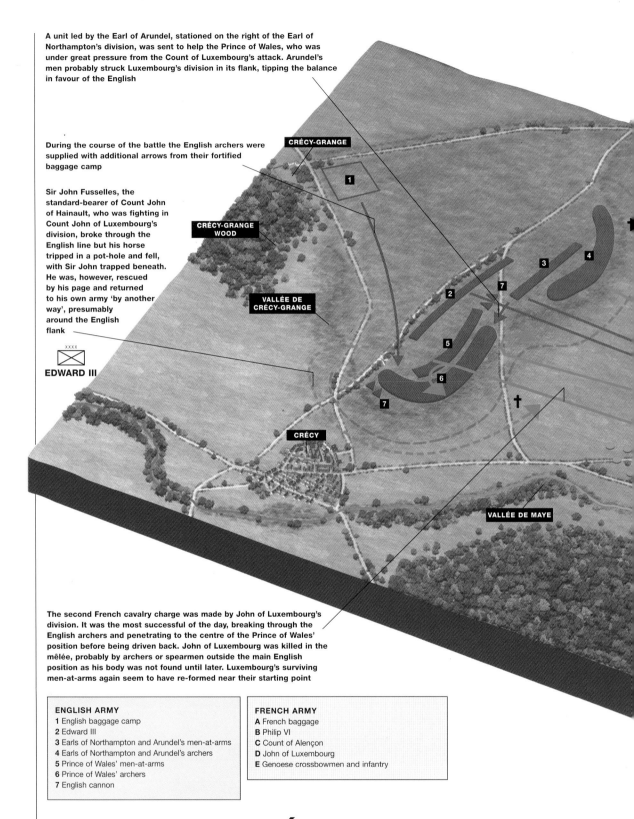

A unit led by the Earl of Arundel, stationed on the right of the Earl of Northampton's division, was sent to help the Prince of Wales, who was under great pressure from the Count of Luxembourg's attack. Arundel's men probably struck Luxembourg's division in its flank, tipping the balance in favour of the English

During the course of the battle the English archers were supplied with additional arrows from their fortified baggage camp

Sir John Fusselles, the standard-bearer of Count John of Hainault, who was fighting in Count John of Luxembourg's division, broke through the English line but his horse tripped in a pot-hole and fell, with Sir John trapped beneath. He was, however, rescued by his page and returned to his own army 'by another way', presumably around the English flank

EDWARD III

CRÉCY-GRANGE

CRÉCY-GRANGE WOOD

VALLÉE DE CRÉCY-GRANGE

CRÉCY

VALLÉE DE MAYE

The second French cavalry charge was made by John of Luxembourg's division. It was the most successful of the day, breaking through the English archers and penetrating to the centre of the Prince of Wales' position before being driven back. John of Luxembourg was killed in the mêlée, probably by archers or spearmen outside the main English position as his body was not found until later. Luxembourg's surviving men-at-arms again seem to have re-formed near their starting point

ENGLISH ARMY
1 English baggage camp
2 Edward III
3 Earls of Northampton and Arundel's men-at-arms
4 Earls of Northampton and Arundel's archers
5 Prince of Wales' men-at-arms
6 Prince of Wales' archers
7 English cannon

FRENCH ARMY
A French baggage
B Philip VI
C Count of Alençon
D John of Luxembourg
E Genoese crossbowmen and infantry

THE BATTLE OF CRÉCY 26 AUGUST 1346:
subsequent French attacks and the English counter-attack

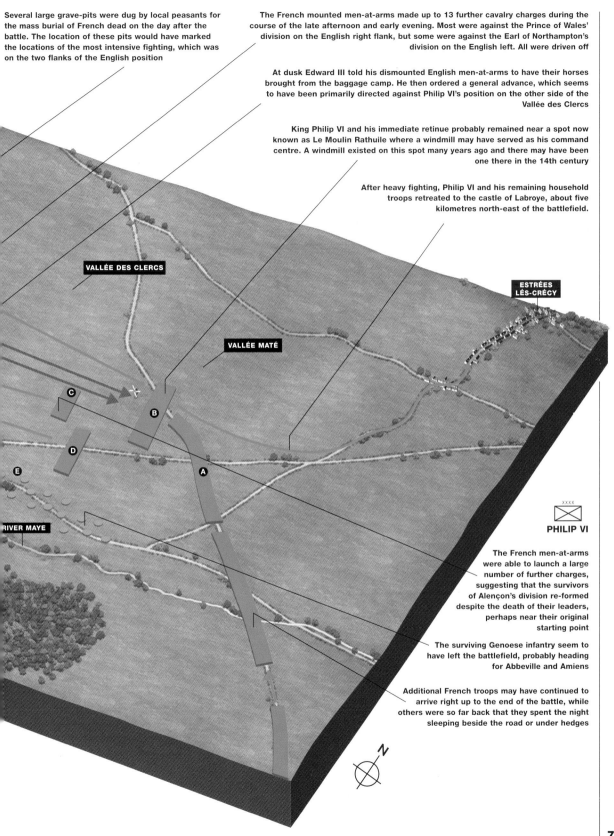

Several large grave-pits were dug by local peasants for the mass burial of French dead on the day after the battle. The location of these pits would have marked the locations of the most intensive fighting, which was on the two flanks of the English position

The French mounted men-at-arms made up to 13 further cavalry charges during the course of the late afternoon and early evening. Most were against the Prince of Wales' division on the English right flank, but some were against the Earl of Northampton's division on the English left. All were driven off

At dusk Edward III told his dismounted English men-at-arms to have their horses brought from the baggage camp. He then ordered a general advance, which seems to have been primarily directed against Philip VI's position on the other side of the Vallée des Clercs

King Philip VI and his immediate retinue probably remained near a spot now known as Le Moulin Rathuile where a windmill may have served as his command centre. A windmill existed on this spot many years ago and there may have been one there in the 14th century

After heavy fighting, Philip VI and his remaining household troops retreated to the castle of Labroye, about five kilometres north-east of the battlefield.

VALLÉE DES CLERCS

VALLÉE MATÉ

ESTRÉES LÉS-CRÉCY

C

B

D

A

E

RIVER MAYE

PHILIP VI

The French men-at-arms were able to launch a large number of further charges, suggesting that the survivors of Alençon's division re-formed despite the death of their leaders, perhaps near their original starting point

The surviving Genoese infantry seem to have left the battlefield, probably heading for Abbeville and Amiens

Additional French troops may have continued to arrive right up to the end of the battle, while others were so far back that they spent the night sleeping beside the road or under hedges

A detail from a carving of the 'Sleeping Guards at the Holy Sepulchre' shows the construction of splinted arm defences and gauntlets. Both were probably made largely of hardened leather. The carving dates from around 1345. (Musée de l'Oeuvre Notre Dame, Strasbourg; author's photograph)

illuminate the battlefield during the first tense hours of night, and the following day many French wagons were burned along with anything the English could not use.

Throughout the night and following foggy morning French soldiers, separated from their leaders, wandered around shouting their passwords as they tried to find their friends. Many were found by the English and all were killed as the victors still took no prisoners. One French contingent of around 2,000 men arrived on the battlefield ignorant of the result, having spent the night on the road from Abbeville. They were militia infantry from Rouen and Beauvais, escorted by Count Louis of Blois and his brother-in law Duke Raoul of Lorraine. Edward III sent Warwick, Suffolk and Northampton against them, to greet them as friends until at the last moment the English charged. The Frenchmen realised their error and fled, though many were killed including Raoul of Lorraine.

The monks of Crécy Grange tended the English wounded. Those who died in their care were buried in an enclosure in the corner of a rough field which was never again ploughed. The English also discovered the full extent of their victory and Edward III ordered Reginald de Cobham to assemble those who could recognise coats-of-arms to identify the dead. No document survives, but according to Jean le Bel the French lost nine princes, 12,000 knights, and from 15,000 to 16,000 others. This was an exaggeration, and even Geoffrey le Baker's estimate of a total of 4,000 noblemen and knights slain on both sides is probably excessive. More realistic is the statement that 1,542 men of aristocratic rank were identified and buried. The literate men who drew up the grisly tally subsequently gave their name to the Vallée des Clercs. A handful of noblemen were extracted for proper burial, some at the Abbey of Valloires, while the rest were tipped into large grave-pits. The death of John of Luxembourg, King of Bohemia, was mourned by both sides. His body was washed, wrapped in linen, placed on a horse-drawn litter and returned to Luxembourg. In his honour the Prince of Wales adopted John of Luxembourg's motto *Ich Dene* or *Ich Dien*, 'I serve', and added beneath it his own badge of three feathers.

Many of Philip VI's most experienced troops had died at Crécy, but instead of trying to rally what remained he retreated to Amiens, where he met Charles, King of the Romans and now of Bohemia, John of Hainault, the Count of Namur and Louis, the new Count of Flanders. Their men had already dispersed so the leaders similarly made their way home. Before doing so, however, Philip VI ordered all the Genoese 'traitors' to be executed. Many were killed before the king's anger cooled and, not surprisingly, the survivors also went home. Philip rode to Pont Saint-Maxence in a secluded part of Hallate Forest about 56 kilometres north of Paris. Meanwhile his son, Duke John of Normandy, finally reach Paris on 8 October, before collecting his father from Pont Saint-Maxence.

AFTERMATH AND RECKONING

After Crécy the English moved slowly northwards, covering only 16 kilometres per day. They stayed close to the coast in hope of receiving supplies by sea, again destroying an area 30 kilometres wide, sacking Étaples and making an unsuccessful assault upon Montreuil-sur-Mer. On 1 September Edward's army rested at Neufchâtel and the following day stopped at Wimille just north of Boulogne to review their situation. The English at Caen had been destroyed by the French garrison in the castle and Edward realised that it was no longer possible to retain Normandy. This was a serious disappointment for those Norman noblemen who had pinned their colours to the English mast. Edward now decided to besiege Calais rather than Boulogne because it would be a better base for future operations and was closer to his Flemish allies.

On 3 September the ancient port of Wissant was destroyed, and on the 4th the vanguard of the English army reached the marshes that surrounded Calais. That day the English fleet also attacked Boulogne but were driven off. They then made contact with King Edward, who wrote a letter home demanding men and material for the forthcoming siege of Calais. A few days later the long-awaited supply fleet arrived from England under the command of Sir John Montgomery. Around this time Godfrey de Harcourt finally abandoned hope of receiving anything from the English and slipped away to Brabant.

The English position as seen from the bottom of the Vallée des Clercs, close to where the Genoese would have started their advance against the Prince of Wales' division on the left of the picture. The modern wooden tower can be seen on the skyline in the centre. (Author's photograph)

THE SECOND FRENCH CHARGE

The first French cavalry attack by the Count of Alençon's division was disrupted by charging through their own infantry crossbowmen and proved a disastrous failure. John, Count of Luxembourg and King of Bohemia, now led his division into the attack, either to help Alençon's retreating men or to take advantage of temporary confusion in the English position. This attack came desperately close to success, penetrating the centre of the Prince of Wales' position and briefly overturning the English banner, while at least one man-at-arms broke right through and out the rear of the English line. Nevertheless, after a bitter struggle the gallant, old and near-blind Count of Luxembourg was killed along with his closest companions and the survivors of his division were forced to retreat.

The view from the Vallée des Clercs towards the left of the English line, held by the earls of Northampton and Arundel. (Author's photograph)

French military failure during the Crécy campaign has been the subject of heated debate on both sides of the Channel. Clearly King Philip's army was not properly arrayed during the battle, their attack started very late in the day and their numerous cavalry charges were poorly co-ordinated. Yet it would be wrong to put all the blame on the French men-at-arms or on the Genoese crossbowmen. The charges were no more disorderly than usual, while the men-at-arms' ability to re-form and return to the attack indicated excellent horsemanship, determination, discipline and control.

The reason for English success most favoured by English historians was the superiority of longbows over crossbows. Carlo Grimaldi himself admitted that the Genoese crossbowmen were outshot by the English longbowmen, while Villani said that the English shot three arrows for every one by the crossbowmen. The longbowmen's ability to outrange the crossbowmen must, however, have been a result of the rain, while the English position above the Genoese enabled them to direct massed falling fire to which the flat trajectory crossbow could not respond.

Skilled English longbowmen now became something of an élite, recruited into English noble households, but there were clear limits to England's new-found military prowess. English armies remained notably good at raiding and major battles, but never achieved the same effectiveness in siege warfare. The psychological impact on the English was significant, however, and their confidence soared. Returning soldiers spread the idea that there were easy pickings in France and although men often had to sell their loot for far less than its true value, Thomas Walsingham could write that: 'The woman was of no account who did

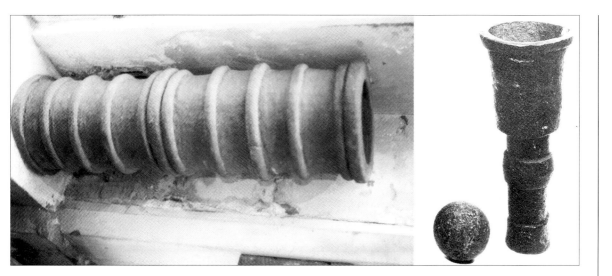

not possess something from the spoils of Caen and Calais and the other cities overseas in the form of clothing, furs, quilts and utensils.'

Changing attitudes made it much easier for Edward III to recruit domestic troops and there were cases of men rising from the humble rank of archer to man-at-arms and captain by the 1350s. King Edward III's victories were also widely seen as evidence of Divine approval for his claims in France, as John Erghome of Yorkshire maintained: 'The Lord God ordains the English to have strength of arms in battles against the French on account of the right which they have in the kingdom of France.' Meanwhile Philip VI was the butt of particular ridicule. To quote the poet Minot: 'In the chambers you are an ornament, in battle almost a

Sir Geoffrey Luttrell with his wife and daughter-in-law, *c.* 1340. The knight is taking his heavy great helm, which could be placed over the lighter bascinet which he already wears. In battle, however, the great helm was rapidly being abandoned. (*Luttrell Psalter*, British Library, Ms. Add. 42130, f. 202v, London)

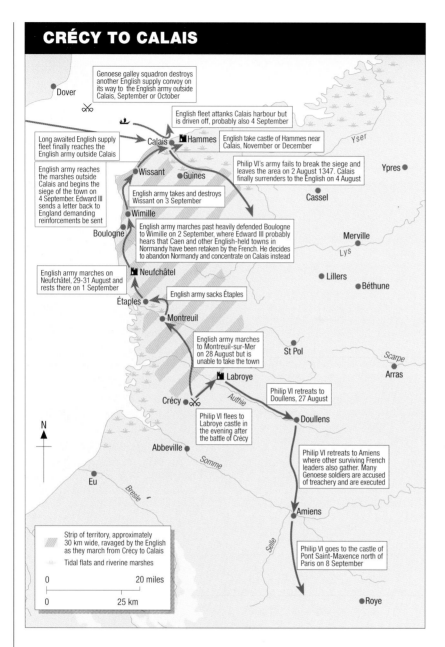

CRÉCY TO CALAIS

Genoese galley squadron destroys another English supply convoy on its way to the English army outside Calais, September or October

English fleet attanks Calais harbour but is driven off, probably also 4 September

Long awaited English supply fleet finally reaches the English army outside Calais

English take castle of Hammes near Calais, November or December

English army reaches the marshes outside Calais and begins the siege of the town on 4 September. Edward III sends a letter back to England demanding reinforcements be sent

Philip VI's army fails to break the siege and leaves the area on 2 August 1347. Calais finally surrenders to the English on 4 August

English army takes and destroys Wissant on 3 September

English army marches past heavily defended Boulogne to Wimille on 2 September, where Edward III probably hears that Caen and other English-held towns in Normandy have been retaken by the French. He decides to abandon Normandy and concentrate on Calais instead

English army marches on Neufchâtel, 29-31 August and rests there on 1 September

English army sacks Étaples

English army marches to Montreuil-sur-Mer on 28 August but is unable to take the town

Philip VI retreats to Doullens, 27 August

Philip VI flees to Labroye castle in the evening after the battle of Crécy

Philip VI retreats to Amiens where other surviving French leaders also gather. Many Genoese soldiers are accused of treachery and are executed

Philip VI goes to the castle of Pont Saint-Maxence north of Paris on 8 September

Dover · Calais · Hammes · Wissant · Guines · Wimille · Boulogne · Neufchâtel · Étaples · Montreuil · Labroye · Crécy · Doullens · Abbeville · Eu · Amiens · Roye

Ypres · Cassel · Merville · Lillers · Béthune · St Pol · Arras

Yser · Lys · Scarpe · Authie · Somme · Bresle · Selle

N

Strip of territory, approximately 30 km wide, ravaged by the English as they march from Crécy to Calais

Tidal flats and riverine marshes

0   20 miles

0   25 km

virgin. Trusting in a tower of deceit, you seek means of defence.' The French themselves were accused of effeminacy, the worst sexual deviations and a strange ability to regain through diplomacy what they lost on the battlefield. Sadly such stereotypes survived long after the end of the Hundred Years War and to some extent can even be found today.

In France the impact of Crécy and the subsequent loss of Calais was political and military. The cavalry learned to be very wary of English longbowmen, not so much for themselves as for their vulnerable horses, and French men-at-arms were soon fighting on foot though their basic tactics remained offensive. Edward III's campaign may have won little territory, only retaining Calais, but it wrought huge damage across northern France and was a political disaster for Philip VI. In psychological terms the impact was the opposite of that seen in England:

Jacob bows before Esau and his followers in the *Velislav Bible*, made around 1340. Once again the military equipment in this Bohemian manuscript is old-fashioned, though the cavalrymen's oval shields may be a distinctive central European style. (University Library, Ms. XXIII-C-24, f.34, Prague)

Crécy was a huge shock for the French nobility and the reputation of the knightly class was severely damaged. The French view of the typical Englishman was, predictably, unflattering: the English were widely regarded as brutish gluttons, the ignoble dregs of mankind. 'Their belly', it was said, 'is their god, and they are zealous in sacrificing to it.' A sense of near despair which gripped France in the wake of Crécy was reflected in a song written by Guillaume de Machaut. He was the greatest French musician of the 14th century but earlier in his life had fought alongside John of Luxembourg in Poland, Italy, Germany and Lithuania. The song was, in fact, a prayer for peace:

> *'Christ, who art the light and the day; cast down by thy power the*
> *vandals who abuse us; prevent us from being downtrodden, by*
> *those who rend us in the wars that have now begun; and from*
> *death, to whose gates we are so near, protect us ... hear the sighs*
> *of the weeping, whom a wretched people is wickedly destroying.*
> *Come, hasten, already our strength is fading.'*

Beyond France the battle of Crécy had less impact on the country's military reputation than might have been expected, though English archers and men-at-arms were soon welcomed as mercenaries in Italy. Carlo Grimaldi, once more the lord of Monaco and leading entrepreneur in the recruitment of Genoese mercenaries, recovered sufficiently to join other expeditions before dying in 1357. His son Ranieri, the lord of nearby Menton, remained a loyal servant of France as did most of the Grimaldi family, and Carlo Grimaldi's descendants rule Monaco to this day.

The Vallée des Clercs seen from just outside Wadicourt. The English held the low ridge on the right, the French and their allies attacking from the trees on the left and from the other side of the valley further left. (Author's photograph)

THE BATTLEFIELDS TODAY

The roads which the English and French armies marched along in Normandy and Picardy still exist. Many of them are, however, minor D-roads or even country tracks because the French started modernising their road network much earlier than did the English. The countryside has, however, changed less in overall terms because France retains the large unhedged fields which were characteristic of the Middle Ages. Forests have diminished, many disappearing or only surviving as scattered woods. Towns and villages have, of course, expanded, though once again France retains a great number of tiny hamlets scattered evenly across the countryside. The city which has changed most is Caen which suffered appalling damage during the Second World War. Otherwise the biggest change is the result of centuries of drainage projects, most notably on low-lying coasts along the eastern base of the Cotentin peninsula, around and to the north of the Somme estuary.

Accommodation is, of course, not a problem in France, and the French network of cheap well equipped camp-sites is probably the best in the world. There are many along the coast of Lower Normandy and sufficient between Paris and the sea. North of Paris they are more scattered before reaching the region around Crécy, the coast of what was Ponthieu, and up the coast of Picardy to Calais. Although the battle was fought close to the small town of Crécy, with another village on its far flank, the ground had only been disturbed to a small extent. The site of the famous windmill is where a small underground reservoir now stands, and in recent years a tall wooden structure, roughly the same size as a medieval windmill, has been erected next to the reservoir. The little town of Crécy does not reach the top of the hill though a school and sports facilities covers part of its south-western slope. The only major structure on the fighting area is a beet processing factory next to where the Vallée des Clercs meets the road from the eastern edge of Crécy. Wadicourt has increased in size but still only abuts the edge of the battlefield. There is also a farm track down the Vallée des Clercs between Wadicourt and the beet factory which can get very muddy.

Several of the campsites near Crécy appear in English guidebooks, the closest probably being at Vironchaux and is certainly well sited for the battlefield. Pleasant bed and breakfast accommodation exists in Crécy, Estrées-les-Crécy and other nearby towns or villages, while larger hotels and excellent restaurants can be found in Abbeville

The superbly carved Easter Sepulchre at Hawton includes several military figures. It was made around 1330 and illustrates English military costume of the period. Note that this man has a brimmed *chapel de fer* over his bascinet. (Hawton Church; author's photograph)

CHRONOLOGY

A longbow archer braces his weapon against his foot as he restrings or unstrings the bow. The English ability to remove and as rapidly replace the strings of their longbows during a sudden rain shower at the start of the battle of Crécy had a major impact on its outcome. (*Luttrell Psalter*, **British Library, Ms. Add. 42130, f. 56r, London**)

1328 Philip of Valois declared King of France as Philip VI.

1337 Start of Hundred Years War.

1340 English defeat French at naval battle of Sluys.

1342 English destroy Genoese galley squadron at Brest; widespread breakdown of order in southern France.

1344 English Parliament votes two-year subsidy for Edward III.

1345 **April,** Edward III offers 'defiance' of Philip VI.

October, English victory at Auberoche in Gascony.

December, English take Aiguillon in Gascony.

December 1345-March 1346, French recruit troops and ships in Genoa, Monaco and Nice.

1346 **18 March,** French start defence measures along Channel coasts.

April, French under Duke of Normandy besiege English-held Aiguillon.

May-June, English army and fleet assembles around Portsmouth.

6 May, Carlo Grimaldi and his fleet leave Nice.

9 June, English defeat Charles of Blois at St Pol de Léon in Brittany.

20 June, Edward III probably decides to invade Normandy; English win small victory at La-Roche Derrien in Brittany.

24 June, leaders of Ghent, Bruges and Ypres agree to support Edward III.

July, Edward orders closing of English ports to stop information reaching France. Carlo Grimaldi's fleet shelters from storms in Tagus estuary, Portugal.

July, Scots raid northern England.

3 July, English fleet attempts to sail from Portsmouth to Normandy but is forced back by contrary winds.

11-12 July, English fleet sails from Portsmouth to Saint-Vaast-la-Hogue on Cotentin peninsula.

12-18 July, English army disembarks at Saint-Vaast-la-Hogue, unsuccessful resistance by Marshal Robert Bertrand. English raid and burn neighbouring towns and villages in Cotentin peninsula.

16 July, English force under Sir Hugh Hastings arrives in Flanders and joins Flemish forces at Ghent; Philip VI receives news of English landing in Normandy.

18 July, English army marches from Saint-Vaast to Valognes.

19 July, English army marches from Valognes to Saint-Côme-du-Mont and Coigny.

20 July, English army takes Carentan.

21 July, English army marches from Carentan to Pont-Hébert.

22 July, English army marches from Pont-Hébert and takes Saint-Lô; Philip VI accepts the Oriflamme sacred banner at Saint-Denis (or on 23rd).

23 July, English army marches from Saint-Lô to Torigny and Cormolain.

24-25 July, English army reaches villages west of Caen; English fleet arrives in Orne estuary after destroying coastal towns and villages.

25 July, Philip VI and available troops move down Seine towards Rouen.

26 July, English seize Caen.

29 July, Edward III sends letter from Caen to Royal Council in England requesting men, supplies and money be sent to Le Crotoy. Philip VI orders general mobilisation with main assembly areas at Paris and Amiens.

30 July, Philip VI and main French force reaches Vernon.

31 July, Philip VI and main French force reach Rouen. Edward III and main English army march from Rouen to Troarn and Argences.

July (end of month), Scots make truce until end of September. Philip VI told of second Flemish invasion threat in north.

August, Genoese fleet arrive in Seine estuary. Ships are beached while crews join army of Philip VI.

1 August, Edward III and main English army march to Rumesnil, Leaupartie and Saint-Pierre-de-Jonque, Anglo-Flemish force leaves Ypres and marches through Bailleul.

2 August, Edward III and main English army march to Lisieux.

2 August, Cardinals sent by Pope to negotiate peace reach Philip VI in Rouen. Anglo-Flemish force clashes with French troops along River Lys.

2-3 August, Philip VI decides to defend line of the Seine, orders and Duke of Normandy to abandon siege of Aiguillon and march to Paris, orders most of troops in Amiens south to Paris. Papal envoys negotiate with Edward III in Lisieux.

4 August, Edward III's army marches from Lisieux to Duranville. Northern French forces gathering at Amiens.

5-6 August, Edward III's army reaches Le Neubourg.

7 August, after council of war Edward III changes direction towards Rouen and reaches Seine at Elbeuf.

8 August, Edward III sends Godfrey de Harcourt to study defences of Rouen. Edward III and English army return to Elbeuf, fail to cross Seine, also fail at Pont-de-l'Arche and march to Louviers. Philip VI and main French army shadow English from north bank of Seine.

9 August, Edward III and English make unsuccessful assault on Vernon.

10 August, English raiding party under Robert de Ferrers crosses Seine and attacks castle of La Roche-Guyon, English army reaches Mounceux and Freneuse, where cardinals return with Philip's offer of peace.

11 August, English bypass French vanguard at Mantes, English attack on Meulan driven off. Rioting in Paris.

The *Liber fiderium* by Sanud was written as a piece of Crusading propaganda, this copy dating from around 1321. It also includes illustrations of military training similar to that undertaken by Philip VI's Genoese crossbowmen. Here, infantrymen train with long spears or pikes in the upper register, while crossbowmen and one figure with a javelin do target practice on the lower register. (Bodleian Library, Ms. Tanner 190, Oxford)

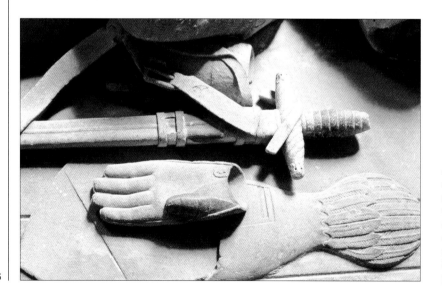

A gauntlet is seen palm upwards on this Alsatian effigy of Ulrich de Huss, the lord of Issenheim, who died in 1344. The small strap and stud may have been to stop the gauntlet coming off too easily in battle. (Musée Unterlinden, Colmar; author's photograph)

12 August, English march through Ecquevilly and Bures.

13 August, Philip VI returns to Paris, establishes headquarters at Saint-Denis.

13-15 August, English rebuilding bridge across Seine at Poissy.

14 August, English from Poissy raid Montjoi, Saint-Cloud, Saint-Germain-en-Laye and Neuilly. Anglo-Flemish force besieges Béthune.

15 August, Philip VI leads French army south of Paris in expectation of battle with Edward III.

16 August, English burn Poissy, send out diversionary raids, cross Seine and march to vicinity of Grisy-les-Plâtres.

17 August, English march north to Auteuil and Vessancourt. Philip VI destroys bridge at Saint-Cloud and probably sends infantry north in pursuit of English.

18 August, English vanguard defeats French force from Amiens near Beauvais; English reach Milly and Troissereux. Philip VI leads cavalry north to Clermont.

19 August, English reach Grandvilliers and Sommereux. French overtake them and advance-guard possibly reaches Amiens.

Defences for the arms and hands developed considerably during the middle part of the 14th century. The carved gauntlets on this effigy, for example, were built up of numerous small pieces of metal presumably riveted to leather gloves. (Ash Church; author's photograph)

20 August, English sack Poix, skirmish with French vanguard. English reach Camps-en-Amienois and Molliens. Philip VI reaches Nampty. Duke of Normandy finally abandons siege of Aiguillon and marches north.

21 August, skirmishing between English and French armies, English only cover ten kilometres.

22 August, English reach Airaines. French main force reaches Amiens, Philip VI orders destruction of bridges across Somme. Edward III sends units to find a bridge but all are broken or strongly defended, attempt to capture bridge at Pont Remy is defeated. French garrison in Béthune makes successful sortie against surrounding Flemings.

23 August, Edward finds Abbeville and Caubert strongly garrisoned so English make a dash for a ford below Abbeville and defeat local militia at Oisemont. Most of English army assembles at Acheux. Philip VI leaves Amiens, reaches Abbeville and Airaines, also sends unit down northern side of Somme towards Le Crotoy.

24 August, English cross Somme by Blanchetaque ford, disperse defenders on north bank, sack Noyelles sur Mer, Le Crotoy and Rue, then camp north of Noyelles. Philip VI and main French force reach ford but are baulked by rising tide. Flemings abandon siege of Béthune and retreat to Merville.

25 August, Edward III learns that Flemings have retreated from Béthune; English establish fortified position north-east of Crécy. Philip VI and French army return to Abbeville; French main force remains in Abbeville and Saint-Riquier as additional contingents arrive.

26 August, English adopt battle array between Crécy and Wadicourt, French march from Abbeville to Crécy, some going via Noyelles. English defeat French at battle of Crécy. Philip VI retreats to castle of Labroye, second French force under Duke of Lorraine and Count of Blois reach Abbeville before continuing march towards Crécy.

27 August, French force under Duke of Lorraine and Count of Blois reach battlefield but are defeated; Philip VI retreats Doullens.

28-31 August, Philip VI retreats to Amiens where surviving French leaders gather. Many Genoese accused of treachery are executed.

28-31 August, English march up coast to Neufchâtel.

2 September, English march to Wimille, Edward III decides to abandon Normandy and concentrate on Calais.

4 September, English reach Calais and begin siege; English fleet attacks Calais but is driven off.

8 September, Philip VI goes to castle of Pont Saint-Maxence.

8 October, Duke of Normandy and his army reach Paris, where soon joined by Philip VI.

1347 **4 August,** Calais surrenders to Edward III.

FURTHER READING

Allmand, C. T., *The Hundred Years War, England and France at War c.1300-c.1450* (Cambridge 1988).

Allmand, C. T., *Society at War, The Experiences of England and France during the Hundred Years War* (revised ed. Woodbridge 1998).

Ashley, W., *Edward III and his wars, 1327-1360* (1887; reprint 1993).

Barnie, J. E., *War in Medieval Society, Social Values and the Hundred Years War 1337-99* (London 1974).

Burne, A. H., *The Crécy War: A Military History of the Hundred Years War from 1337 to the Peace of Bretigny* 1360 (London 1955).

Chazelas, A., *Documents Relatifs au Clos de Galées de Rouen at aux Armées de Mer du Roi de France de 1293 à 1418* (Paris 1977-78).

Contamine, P., *'Crecy (1346) et Azincourt (1415): une comparaison,'* in *Divers aspects du Moyen Age in Occident; Actes du Congres tenu a Calais en Septembre 1974* (Calais 1977) 29-44.

Contamine, P., (ed.), *Guerre et Société en France, en Angleterre et en Bourgogne XIVe-XVe Siècle* (Lille 1991).

Contamine, P., *Guerre, Etat et Société á la Fin du Moyen Age: Etudes sur les Armées des rois de France 1337-1494* (Paris 1972).

Curry, A. and Hughes M. (eds), *Arms, Armies and Participants in the Hundred Years War* (Woodbridge 1994).

Devries, K., *Infantry warfare in the early fourteenth century: Discipline, tactics and technology* (1996).

Froissart, J. (J. Jolliffe ed. and trans.), *Froissart's Chronicles* (London 1967).

Hewitt, H. J., *The Organisation of War under Edward III, 1338-62* (Manchester 1966).

Huguet, A., *'Aspects de la Guerre de Cent Ans en Picardie maritime,'* *Memoires de la Societé des Antiquaires de Picardie,* XLVIII (1941) and L (1944).

Jean de Venette (J. Birdsall trans., R.A. Newhall ed.), *The Chronicle of Jean de Venette* (New York 1953).

Lot., F., *L'Art Militaire et les Armées au Moyen Age en Europe et dans le Proche Orient* (Paris 1946).

Louandre, F-C., *L'histoire d'Abbeville et du comté de Ponthieu* (Paris 1944; revised 1983).

Lucas, H. S., *Low Countries and the Hundred Years War, 1326-1347* (Ann Arbor 1929).

Palmer, J. J. N., (ed.), *Froissart: Historian* (Totowa NJ 1981).

Perroy, E., *The Hundred Years War* (London 1951).

Postan, M. M., *'The Costs of the Hundred Years War,'* *Past and Present XXVII* (1964) 34-53.

Prestwich, M., *The Three Edwards: War and State in England 1272-1377* (London 1981).

Prince A. E., *'The Payment of Army Wages in Edward III's Reign,'* *Speculum*, XIX (1944) 137-160.

Prince A. E., *'The Strength of English Armies in the Reign of Edward III,'* *The English Historical Review CLXXXIII* (1931) 353-371.

Sumption, J., *The Hundred Years War, vol. I: Trial by Battle* (London 1990).

Thompson, P. E. (ed.), *Contemporary Chronicles of the Hundred Years War* (London 1966).

Wailly, H. de*, Crécy 1346: Anatomy of a battle* (Poole 1987).

The Cross of John of Luxembourg, on the road between Crécy and Fontaine-sur-Maye, is said to mark the spot where he died. This is, however, unlikely as his body and those of his companions were found on the battlefield, with their horses' bridles still tied together. The cross clearly became associated with him at an early date, perhaps because he and his men rode past as they advanced against the English position. (Author's photograph)

INDEX

GLOSSARY

akheton A padded jerkin worn under plate armour.
arrière ban French general levy of soldiers. (pp.22-23)
aventail A protective collar lacing up to cover the throat and
  lower face. (p.21)
ballock dagger A dagger with two small swellings at the base of
  the grip. (p.57)
banneret A knight leading a body of men under his own banner.
  (p.21)
bascinet A helmet. (pp.29, 46, 84)
bevor A helmet.
bombard A cannon. (pp.53, 57, 81)
centar An officer leading 100 men.
chamfron Protective head-armour for a horse. (p.37)
chapel de fer A brimmed metal helmet. (p.84)
chevauchée A swift-moving mounted raid or invasion.
coat of plates Form of armour. (p.20)
cote d'armes An overgarment bearing the symbolic design
  particular to the wearer, his coat of arms.
crossbow See pp. 26-27 and 31.
dard Javelin.
destrier A heavy war-horse. (p.21)
falchion A weapon like a cleaver.
fingers, three Defiant English archers would show their enemies
  the centre three fingers of their bow-drawing hand in a
  threatening gesture. The modern version employs two fingers.
gauntlet Armoured glove.

glaive A mounted man-at-arms with his retinue. (p.24)
gorget Plate armour protecting the throat.
great helm A bucket-like cover-all helmet.
halberd A weapon comprised of a shaft with a combined axe and
  spike head. (p.21)
hauberk Chain mail body armour. (p.29)
herce, of archers See p.53.
indenture A system of raising troops. (p.15)
lance A weapon, but also a group of mounted men led by a
  man-at-arms. (p.24)
longbow See pp.18-19, 21 and 57.
lorigone A mail hauberk. (p.29)
misericord dagger A dagger with a projecting disc at the base of
  the grip.
Oriflamme The sacred Royal war banner of the French. (p.43)
pavise A long shield, often with a point at the bottom for sticking
  in the ground. A protection for crossbowmen carried by
  pavesarii. (p.18)
poleaxe An axe-head mounted on a shaft or pole. (p.21)
pot helm A helmet.
purveyance A system of forced sale of supplies. (p.16)
quarrel A bolt, a missile fired from a crossbow. (p.30)
vervelles Rivets around a helmet to which the aventail is secured.
vintenar An officer leading twenty men.
vrysoun A helmet covering. (p.21)
Wardrobe An administrative department. (p.16)

PLACES TO VISIT

Lying between Calais and the Somme and just east of the A16 Autoroute are a number of places of interest to the military historian: Montreuil-sur-Mer, Agincourt, Hesdin, Crécy-en-Ponthieu and Abbeville. Both Montreuil and Hesdin are pleasing little towns with a range of hotels and restaurants, while Abbeville offers all the facilities of a larger town.

Crécy-en-Ponthieu

Office de Tourisme de Crécy-en-Ponthieu
Location: 32, rue du Maréchal Leclerc, 80150 Crécy-en-Ponthieu, France
Tel: 00 33 (0) 22 23 93 84. Out of season: 00 33 (0) 22 23 54 43
The tourist information office is in the centre of the village, near the *Lanterne des Morts*, and can give details of Chambres d'Hôtes (B&Bs), hotels and restaurants, as well as booklets and other information about the battle.

The probable site of the windmill on the D111 to Wadicourt is now crowned with a fine wooden tower, three floors high, with a helical

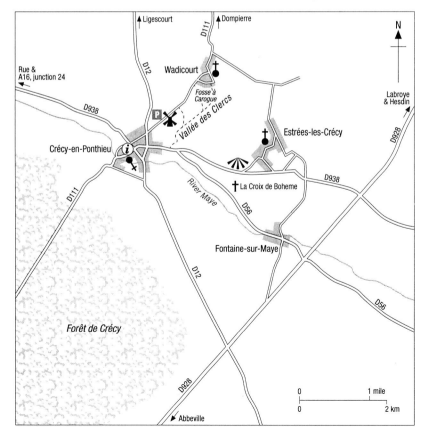

Map of tourist sites in and around Crécy.

CRÉCY

VIEWING TOWER

staircase offering an easy climb to overlook the field of battle. The modest car park (one coach and half a dozen car spaces, picnic tables and W.C. open in summer season) is on the other side of the narrow road up which drivers accelerate hard. Take care and remember which side of the road they drive on when looking out! Compare the view from the tower with the bird's-eye views on pages 54-5 and 66-7, and the photos on pages 56, 61, 63 and 64.

Those who like to walk should take note of the recent weather as the paths and tracks get very wet and muddy. Along the road to Wadicourt a track leads down the hill to the right into the Vallée des Clercs in a dog-leg easily seen in the panoramic picture above. Along the bottom of the valley a track goes to the road next to the factory on the edge of Crécy (making it possible to walk back to the village) and, in the other direction, to Wadicourt. Looking up (see photo page 77), and climbing up towards the windmill shows what the attackers were up against; no joke on wet, slippery ground with arrows raining down. Driving along the high ground from the view tower to Wadicourt on the D111 brings you to another track down into the valley from which the gully that protected the English left, the *Fosse á Carogne*, can be seen (between this viewpoint and the track going into Wadicourt next to the church). At the northern exit from Wadicourt a narrow road goes right and a right at the next junction brings you into Estrées-les-Crécy. Head for the most westerly junction with the main road back into Crécy, and, just before the junction, the road widens next to a calvary, a traveller's shrine, giving room to park. The field to the west, towards the battlefield, is higher than the road but a sloping track leads up to the point at which the panoramic photo of the English position was taken.

DOG-LEG TRACK

The English position from the outskirts of Estrées. From the left, buildings on the edge of Crécy, the viewing tower on the skyline, the dog-leg track into the valley which cannot be seen fully from here (it is deeper than it appears) and the road to Wadicourt. The main French positions were in the middle ground.

This could approximate to the French command position. From here it looks easy! The viewing tower can be seen on the far ridge.

The French approached from the south, crossing the River Maye west of Fontaine-sur-Maye. On the D56 which connects the village to Crécy a monument to John of Luxembourg, King of Bohemia, stands close to the probable river-crossing point. Further south the forest still covers a huge area and offers lovely walks and excellent picnic places.

South and West of Crécy

In the town of Rue, to the west, the other side of the Autoroute, is a museum devoted to the brothers René and Gaston Caudron, the creators of one of the leading French aircraft of the First World War, the Caudron 3.

Immediately south-west of Abbeville the Monts de Caubert tower overlooks both the town and the country further south. On top is a huge cross of Lorraine, a memorial to the dead of both World Wars and nearby the concrete fixings for German anti-aircraft guns, now obscured by grass. It was against German positions here that Brigadier-general Charles de Gaulle launched his last field action on 4 June 1940.

The Canal de la Somme now allows shipping access to Abbeville, but the probable site of Blanchetaque can be visited on the road from Gouy via the lock at Petit Port to the D40 between Abbeville and Port-le-Grand.

At Noyelles-sur-Mer, on the way to William the Conqueror's point of departure for England in 1066, St Valery-sur-Somme, Chinese labourers of the First World War are buried in their own, specially designed, cemetery.

North of Crécy

The town of Hesdin was a fortified Spanish holding until Louis XIII regained it in 1639. The information office in the Place d'Armes, the main square where you can park, is very useful.

To the north-west, along the River Canche, is the hill-top town of Montreuil-sur-Mer. No longer on the sea-shore, it still has a complete circuit of medieval walls to explore, numerous hotels and restaurants and, in the main square, a statue of General Haig, for it was here that the British had their headquarters in the First World War.